W9-CFO-766

● Cultural China Series

Wei Liming Chinese
Festivals

Translated by Yue Liwen & Tao Lang

CHINA
INTERCONTINENTAL
PRESS

图书在版编目（CIP）数据

中国节日 / 韦黎明编著；乐利文，陶郎译. —北京：五
洲传播出版社，2005.10
ISBN 7-5085-0836-X

I. 中...
II. ①韦... ②乐... ③陶...
III. 节日—风俗习惯—中国—英文
IV. K892.1

中国节日

编 著 者	韦黎明
译　　者	乐利文　陶　郎
责任编辑	邓锦辉
整体设计	海　洋
出版发行	五洲传播出版社（北京海淀区北小马厂6号　邮编:100038）
设计制作	北京锦绣东方图文设计有限公司
承 印 者	北京华联印刷有限公司
版　　次	2005年10月第1版
印　　次	2005年10月第1次印刷
开　　本	720×965毫米　1/16
印　　张	8.5
字　　数	90千字
印　　数	1-8500册
书　　号	ISBN 7-5085-0836-X/K·718
定　　价	90.00元

图片提供:Imaginechina、国务院新闻办图片库（署名者除外）

Table of Contents

Chinese Festivals

China is a country with a long history of about 5,000 years. In its ever-forward history course there have developed a good number of traditional festivals which are of rich varieties and long standing. The culture of festivals rooted deeply in the people, and it thus shows its enormous vitality. In spite of the change of times, it has gradually become part of the heritages of the colorful Chinese culture.

The generation and development of festivals is a course of their shaping, perfecting and then their gradual integrating with the social life. It is the result of the social development which has reached a certain stage. The increasing productive force of the society, the ever-improving conditions of people's life, and the emergence and frequence of the religious activities has all provided a stage for the emerging and developing of festivals. Most of the traditional festivals in ancient China had something to do with the development of astronomy, calendar and mathematics. The beginning of these traditional festivals was particularly related to the later decided 24 seasonal division points under the traditional Chinese lunar calendar. All of the 24 seasonal divisions had almost been settled by the time of Han Dynasty (206 BC-AD 220). These

"Joyful Peasants," New Year poster. Absolutely different festivals and customs can be formed on the basis of traditional agricultural production.

"Busy peasants" and "Busy peasant women," New Year posters of Yangjiabu, late-Qing Dynasty.

divisions helped to form festivals, for in their work and life, people developed different customs and activities which can express their good wishes according to the yearly change of seasons and natural phenomena. Based on these customs and activities, festivals began to take their shapes.

A large part of the Chinese festivals had already showed the rudiment in the Qin Dynasty (221-206 BC), such as the New Year's Eve, New Year's Day, Lantern Festival, *Shangsi* Festival, *Hanshi* Festival, Dragon Boat Festival, Double Seventh Festival, and Double Ninth Festival. However, the shaping and spread of

Twenty-Four Seasonal Division Points

Season	Division points	Solar calendar	Lunar calendar	Ecliptic (degree)	Significance
Spring	Beginning of Spring	4-5 Feb.	Early first lunar month	315	Spring begins
	Rain Water	19-20 Feb.	Middle first lunar month	330	The amount of rain increases
	Waking of Insects	5-6 Mar.	Early second lunar month	345	The hibernated animals are awoken by the spring thunder
	Vernal Equinox	20-21 Mar.	Middle second lunar month	0	The sun shines above the Equator and the day and night go halves
	Pure Brightness	5-6 Apr.	Early third lunar month	15	Pure and bright; trees and grass thriving
	Grain Rain	20-21 Apr.	Middle third lunar month	30	The rainfall begins to increase and grains grow well
Summer	Beginning of Summer	5-6 May	Early fourth lunar month	45	Summer begins
	Grain Budding	21-22 May	Middle fourth lunar month	60	Grains begin to be in the milk
	Grain in Ear	6-7 Jun.	Early fifth lunar month	75	Awny crops like wheat begin to ripe
	Summer Solstice	21-22 Jun.	Middle fifth lunar month	90	The sun shines above the Tropic of Cancer and the day reaches its longest time
	Slight Heat	7-8 Jul.	Early sixth lunar month	105	Hot
	Great Heat	23-24 Jul.	Middle sixth lunar month	120	The hottest time
Autumn	Beginning of Autumn	7-8 Aug.	Early seventh lunar month	135	Autumn begins
	Limit of Heat	23-24 Aug.	Middle seventh lunar month	150	The summer-heat begin to die down
	White Dew	7-8 Sep.	Early eighth lunar month	165	Getting cold and dews begin to show up in the morning
	Autumnal Equinox	23-24 Sep.	Middle eighth lunar month	180	The sun shines above the Equator and the day and night go halves
	Cold Dew	8-9 Oct.	Early ninth lunar month	195	Getting colder and the morning dew is very cool
	Frost's Descent	23-24 Oct.	Middle ninth lunar month	210	Getting colder and frost begin to show up

(*continued*)

Season	Division points	Solar calendar	Lunar calendar	Ecliptic (degree)	Significance
Winter	Beginning of Winter	7-8 Nov.	Early tenth lunar month	225	Winter begins
	Slight Snow	22-23 Nov.	Middle tenth lunar month	240	Slight snowfalls
	Great Snow	7-8 Dec.	Early eleventh lunar month	255	Great snowfalls
	Winter Solstice	22-23 Dec.	Middle eleventh lunar month	270	Sun shines above the Tropic of Capricorn and the day reaches its shortest time
	Slight Cold	5-6 Jan.	Early twelfth lunar month	285	Cold
	Great Cold	20-21 Jan.	Middle twelfth lunar month	300	Extremely cold

the customs has gone through a long time of development. The primal customs were related to the primitive worship and some superstitions and they often had something to do with the colorful legends and stories, which have covered a romantic veil on the festivals. The religion also influenced the festivals to a certain extent. Some historical figures, after merging into the culture of festivals, also became more memorable in the history. All these factors have contributed to the profound historic and cultural charm of festivals.

By the time of Han Dynasty, the major traditional Chinese festivals had been settled to a large extent. The Han Dynasty was the first golden period after the great union of the whole country. At that time, the nation was in a stable position in terms of political and economic life and the science and technology were developing rapidly. Regional cultures such as the cultures of Qin, Chu and Qi-Lu, which had had a long history, integrated with each other in such a historic way that they finally formed a cultural community, which is represented by the culture of Han nationality. The factors above helped to create social and cultural conditions for the finalization of festivals.

Coming to the Tang Dynasty (618-907), the festivals had stripped off its mysterious coat of primitive sacrifices and superstitions and changed into more entertaining amusement. Many relaxing activities appeared and soon prevailed as a kind of fashion. Festivals became so joyful and colorful that they really became happy events. Owing to the communication between different nationalities and the development of religions, new vigor was always being infused into the culture of festivals, and the customs are able to last till today.

The traditional Chinese festivals not only are an important part of the cultural life of the Chinese people, but they also play a special role in the commercial trade and cultural communication. Almost every festival is the day of trading and communicating. In these festivals, farmers exchange different products; townspeople improve their living conditions by purchasing goods; scholars share their works with each other; and the government also hold some grand activities to establish or reaffirm the moral principles as a kind of conduction.

The generation and development of traditional festivals is a long course of the accumulation of a nation's historical culture. The strong cohesion and considerable comprehension of traditional Chinese festivals is just in accord with the rich and colorful history of Chinese nation. China has a lot of ethnic groups. Apart from some important traditional festivals of Han nationality, the other fifty-five ethnic groups also have their own peculiar festivals and customs. People today can easily make out an exciting picture of ancient people's social lives through the customs of festivals that originated from the ancient time and last till today. Getting close and even into the culture of these colorful festivals, you can get in touch with the essence of the Chinese culture.

Due to the development of society and the advancement of times, people's views about life have changed greatly, and the culture of Chinese festivals is changing with time, too. Since the Revolution of 1911, China entered a phase where different styles of festivals co-existed with each other. Some of them rose and some of them fell. On the one hand, a few important ones, the four major festivals (the Spring Festival, Pure Brightness Festival, Dragon Boat Festival and Mid-Autumn Festival) in particular, are still widely celebrated among people. Not only did they

The couple of golden wedding are presenting roses to each other for a romantic Valentine's Day.

inherit the essence of the culture of traditional festivals, but they also developed more forms and took in some new elements of the new time. Some less important festivals, on the other hand, were gradually forgotten and had faded over the years. Recently some western festivals were introduced into China, and these "foreign festivals" such as Valentine's Day, Fools' Day, Mothers' Day and Christmas Day are becoming more and more popular among the Chinese people, especially the city youngsters.

As people's living conditions keep improving and their lifestyles change gradually, the ways of celebrating the festivals have changed, too. Combining both tradition and fashion, they show a trend of diversification. A large number of people stick to the traditional customs no more and begin to choose a more simple and casual way to celebrate the festivals. Some new stuff drew people's attention: the Internet and short messages have brought a brand-new way of expressing good wishes between people. The Chinese festivals and the festival life of the Chinese people are getting more and more colorful and exciting.

The festivals introduced in this book are only a little part of the numerous and rich Chinese festivals, though they will provide an entry to the charming Chinese folk cultures.

A beautifully decorated Christmas tree outside a shopping mall.

Traditional Festivals

China covers a large area and consists of a number of ethnic groups. Different areas and ethnic groups have formed different customs concerning food, clothing, shelter and transport, festivals, courtesies, sacrifices and religion, weddings and funerals. All of these customs have lasted for hundreds of years and have become part of the culture of different areas and ethnic groups. At the same time, some of them become the festivals and customs shared by all the Chinese people and merged into the traditional Chinese culture.

Laba Festival

Name: *Laba* Festival
Date: the eighth day of the twelfth lunar month

In China, the twelfth month of lunar year is called "*la* month," and the eighth day of the twelfth lunar month is thus called "*Laba* Festival" (eight reads *ba* in Chinese) or "*la* day." *Laba* Festival is a traditional festival of Han nationality. It is also regarded as the prelude to the Spring Festival.

It is recorded that *Laba* Festival originated from the ancient Chinese *la* ceremony. The Chinese people have always paid great attention to agriculture ever since the ancient time. Whenever there was a bumper harvest, the ancient people would regard it as the result of all gods' bless, so they would hold a grand ceremony to celebrate the harvest, which was called a "*la* ceremony." After the ceremony people would entertain their fellow villagers with the porridge that were made of their newly gained broomcorn millet. Everybody would get together to enjoy the festival. The *la* ceremony later developed into a festival mainly to commemorate the ancestors. In the 5th century, the government decided that the eighth day of the twelfth lunar month is the *Laba* Festival.

After the spread of Buddhism into China, people made up another story based on the traditional custom of honoring the ancestors and eating porridge, saying that the eighth day of the twelfth lunar month was the day when Sakyamuni, the founder of Buddhism, became a Buddha. The story goes that Sakyamuni had practiced Buddhism for many years and the hunger turned him into just a bag of bones and he intended to give up. Right at that time a shepherd girl helped him with rice and porridge, which restored energy into him and brought him into the right track of thought. Contemplating under the bodhi tree, he finally became a Buddha on the eighth day of the twelfth lunar month. To commemorate this event, the Buddhists began to make porridge with rice and dried fruits to make offerings to the Buddha on that day every year, and the porridge was called "*laba* porridge."

The Chinese have been **eating *laba* porridge** for over one thousand years ever since the Song Dynasty (960-1279). At that time, the central and local government as well as the monasteries would make *laba* porridge on every *Laba* Festival. This custom became particularly popular in the Qing Dynasty (1644-1911). The emperor, empress and princes would grant *laba* porridge to their officials and servants and send rice and fruits to the monasteries. All the families would make *laba* porridge to honor their ancestors, too. People not only got together to enjoy the food with their family members but also shared their food with other families to show their good wishes.

There are all kinds of *laba* porridge. The traditional *laba* porridge should include eight main materials and eight supplementary materials, which accord with the "*ba*" in "*laba* porridge" and suggests good luck. ("*Ba*," in Chinese, is usually related to "*fa*," which means prosperity.) The main materials usually consist of beans like red beans, mung beans, cowpeas, haricots, peas and broad beans and grain like rice, millet, polished round-grained rice, sticky rice, wheat, oat, corn and broomcorn. People can choose what he prefers from these materials. The supplementary materials can usually be chosen from preserved peach, preserved apricot, walnuts, jujube paste, chestnuts,

Two "Old Beijingers" enjoying laba *porridge.*

11

persimmons, melon seeds, lotus seeds, peanuts, hazels, pine nuts, preserved pear and raisins.

After choosing the main materials, it is time to put them into a pot full of water and cook them on a slow fire. When all these have been done, some sweet seasonings like sugar, rose and sweet osmanthus will be added into it. The *laba* porridge varies in different areas in China, and the most delicate one is in Beijing. There are more types of fruits in the rice, such as jujube, lotus seeds, nuts, chestnuts, almonds, pine nut kernels, longans, hazels, raisins, water chestnuts, roses, red beans and peanuts, summing up to more than twenty types.

People usually began to get busy since the night of the seventh day in that month. They wash the rice, steep the fruits in water for some time, pick out the good ones, peel them, get rid of the kernels and finally began to cook all these materials from midnight. After that, the slow fire will keep them until the next morning when the *laba* porridge is finally done.

If the family is very particular about the festival, they will pay special attention to the color of the porridge. All the deep-colored beans will not be taken into consideration. Only polished glutinous rice, seeds of Job's tears, water-nuts and lotus seeds are chosen as the materials and made into porridge. The white porridge placed in exquisite dishware is not only delicious but also good-looking. Moreover, it is also an indication of good luck and bumper harvest. The Chinese think that it is a very agreeable scene to have the whole family gathering at the table and eating the delicious *laba* porridge. Families which are even more particular about the festival will carve the fruits into shapes of people or animals and knead the food with colors such as jujube paste, bean paste, tomatoes and haw jelly cakes into the figures in the legends. This kind of *laba* porridge, however, can only be seen on the altar tables of some big monasteries.

When the *laba* porridge is done, it should first be offered to gods and ancestors as the sacrifice. Next will be the relatives and friends, and the porridge must be sent out by noon. Finally the whole family will enjoy it together. The leftover *laba* porridge, even if it is left after several days, is considered as a good omen since it suggests that there will be leftovers every year. What's

Steeping laba *garlic.*

more, if you share the porridge with the needed people, it will be seen as an accumulation of virtue.

Besides cooking *laba* porridge, people in northern China also have the habit of making "**laba garlic**" on *Laba* Festival. The housewives peel the garlic, put it in jars and fill the jars with vinegar. Then these jars are sealed on the *Laba* Festival and placed in some warm room. When it comes to the New Year's Eve and the family is ready to eat *jiaozi*, the garlic will be brought to the table. The vinegar-soaked garlic cloves take on a jade-like green color, which is rather beautiful in contrast with the red vinegar and can greatly improve the atmosphere of the festival.

Preliminary Year

Name: Preliminary Year (*Xiao Nian*)
Date: the 23rd day of the last lunar month

Twenty-third of the last lunar month, or "preliminary year," is a day when people offer sacrifices to the kitchen god.

The "monarch of kitchen" or "kitchen god," who is worshiped among the Chinese

"Kitchen God," New Year poster.

people, is a god who takes charge of the fortune of families. It is said that on the 23rd day of the twelfth lunar month every year, the kitchen god will report to Yuhuang Dadi (Jade Emperor, supreme deity in Taoism) about the goods and evils of each family so that Yuhuang Dadi can decide whether they should be awarded or punished. Therefore, when it is the time to send the kitchen god off, people will put candies, water, soybeans and fodder in front of his statue. The last three are prepared for the horse with which the kitchen god goes to heaven. When giving offerings to him, people will melt the *Guandong* candy (a kind of candy originated in Northeast China) and apply it to the kitchen god's mouth. With his mouth being glued, he will not be able to speak ill of others before Yuhuang Dadi. People follow the custom that "men don't worship moon and women don't revere kitchen." Therefore the ceremony of offering sacrifices to the kitchen god is only hold by men.

On the New Year's Eve, the kitchen god will come to earth with other gods to celebrate the Spring Festival, so there should be a ceremony of "welcoming the kitchen god."

People always began to **clean their houses** from the eighth

"Door Gods," New Year poster of Yangliuqing, Tianjin, Qing Dynasty.

day of the twelfth lunar month and it usually lasts until the 23rd day. The cleaning is also called house cleaning or dusting. It is a thorough cleaning of the house, which aims to get rid of the bad luck and take on a new look. Every family will do the cleaning carefully and completely to make the house bright and clean. Twenty-fourth day of the last lunar month is decided as the "house cleaning day" in Beijing. Every year when it comes to that day, the housewives will firstly cover the beds and furniture and hood themselves. Then they will brush the walls with brooms. Later on they will clean the tables and floors. After all these, every family will take an entirely new look.

Spring Festival

Name: Spring Festival (*Chun Jie* in Chinese pronunciation)
Date: the first day of the first lunar month

Every year when winter is about to end and spring is coming, the Chinese always grandly celebrate the first traditional festival in a year – the Spring Festival (New Year of lunar calendar). It can be called the grandest and most exciting festival for the Chinese, containing a long history and rich cultural connotations.

Lion dancing during the Spring Festival.

Spring festival is the beginning of lunar year, commonly called *Guo Nian*. In the long history of over 2,000 years, Chinese New Year customs have undergone a developing process of germination, formation, change, and transition.

Pre-Qin period is the germinating time of New Year customs. At that time, people held celebrations after agricultural affairs were finished as a sacrificial activity to thank gods' bestowment. "July," *The Book of Songs*, records the festive customs at the turn of two years in the period of Western Zhou (1046-771 BC), when people offered luscious wind and lamb to gods as reward for their blessing and obligation during the past year and as invocation for favorable weather and bumper harvest in the oncoming year. There was not a fixed date for these celebrations because different states used different calendars. But it's around

15

大過新年

"Celebrating the New Year," New Year poster. Provided by Li Lulu.

the time in winter when agriculture was not so busy. It is the embryo of New Year customs in later generations.

New Year customs were finalized in Han Dynasty. After the social tumult at the end of Warring States (475-221 BC) and Qin Dynasty, government of Western Han (206 BC-AD 25) adopted "Rehabilitation" policy in its early time, which recovered and developed the social production and restored social order. People were more hopeful about their life and so a series of festive customs got to be formed. The adoption of *Taichu Calendar* stabilized calendar system for a long time, so the first day of the first lunar month as the first day of a year was settled. As a result, god worshipping, sacrificing and celebrating activities that used to be held at different time in late winter or early spring were gradually unified to be held on the first day of the first lunar month. With the development of times, New Year customs on the first day of the first lunar month were getting more and more interesting from Han Dynasty to Southern and Northern dynasties (420-589). People played fireworks, changed Spring Festival couplets, drank *tusu* wine (ancient wine of China), stayed up all night on New Year's Eve, enjoyed lanterns, etc. Spring festival gradually developed into the most important festival in China.

New Year customs were changed in Tang Dynasty. Tang is a time of economic prosperity and political flourishing as well as frequent intercourse between Chinese and foreign cultures. New Year customs, by and by, came out of the mystic atmosphere of invocation, superstition, and evil prevention, but changed into entertaining and ceremonial celebrations. Crackers on New Year were no longer a means of keeping away ghosts and preventing evil, but were ways of joy and fun. The focus of New Year celebration shifted from god worship to entertainments for people, and to people's own recreation and enjoyment of life. Therefore it is safe to say that only after Tang Dynasty has new year really become a "happy festival and blessing day" for all.

New Year customs were transited in Ming (1368-1644) and Qing dynasties, which were mainly reflected in two aspects. First, their ceremonial and social function increased. On New Year, people visited each other; high officials gave each other their cards or went to each other's houses. Common people paid attention to reciprocal courtesy, too, presenting gifts and paying New Year visits to one another. Second, their recreational function increased. During the period of New Year, all kinds of recreations were carried out – lion dance, dragon dance, drama playing, story telling, high stilts playing, land boats racing, etc., rich and colorful. Beijingers visited Changdian, Guangzhou people went to flower market, Suzhou people listened to the toll of Hanshan Temple, Shanghai people went to Town God's Temple... Recreations at different places possessed their own characteristics and different entertainments kept coming on, making people dazed and excited. New Year customs at that time fully absorbed Chinese traditional culture, becoming a

The Qing-Dynasty New Year poster, "Liannian Youyu (Surplus Every Year)," expresses a good expectation for the coming year.

17

Chinese Festivals

The red Fus (good fortune) are usually pasted on doors or windows for auspicious happiness.

folk-custom exposition where Chinese customs and traditions that had had thousands of years of history were displayed in a centralized way.

During the period of New Year, which is a traditional festival, Han nationality and most minor nationalities of China hold various celebrations, which mostly feature sacrifice to god or Buddha, memorial sacrifice to ancestors, ridding the old and welcoming and new, embracing joy and receiving fortune, and invocation for a good year. These celebrations are of varied forms and with full national characteristics.

In the past 2,000 and more years, the splendid celebration of New Year prevails in China. It almost penetrates everyone's life and moulds the soul of every Chinese all over the world. Every time when it comes to the end of lunar year, people who are away from home hurry home to be with their families, and interesting new-year customs like staying up for the New Year, making *jiaozi*, posting New Year couplets, making New Year visits, and many other things have become common habits of all Chinese people. The Spring Festival customs of the Chinese have also radiated to neighboring countries like Vietnam, North Korea, South Korea, Japan, etc. They celebrate New Year in similar ways.

Spring Festival is not just one day but includes many

activities in the first lunar month. For the Chinese, Spring Festival celebration only comes to a rest after the 15th day of the first lunar month, when the Lantern Festival is spent. In fact, people start preparing for Spring Festival celebration from as early as the 23rd of the last lunar month of the previous year. During this time, all families are busy with overall cleaning, making special purchases for the festival, sticking paper-cuts on windows, hanging New Year posters, writing New Year couplets, cooking rice cakes, and making all sorts of foods, all in preparation to get rid of the old and welcome in the new. The night before New Year is called New Year's Eve, which is an essentially important time for family gathering. Family members sit around a table, enjoy a sumptuous Hogmanay dinner, and then sit together to chat or play. Most of them stay up all night until next dawn, which is called *Shou Sui* in Chinese (waiting for New Year).

Shou Sui means not to sleep on the last night of a year and to stay up all night to welcome a new year. There is an interesting story among common folks for many generations about this origin of the custom. In time immemorial, a kind of fierce and strange beast lived in deep mountains and thick forests that people called Nian (Chinese for year). It had a ferocious appearance and savage character, eating everything from snap bug to living humans and changing its diet everyday, which makes people change color on hearing its name Nian. Later, people got to know the regularity of Nian's activities. Every 365 days it went to a human community to eat them, and it usually appeared after sunset and would go back to mountain or forest

(Left) *Staying up late until daybreak on New Year's Eve to welcome the new year. Painted by Sheng Xishan.*
(Right) *Having dumplings for the New Year is a tradition in many Chinese families. Painted by Sheng Xishan.*

when roosters crowed dawn.

Counting the exact date of Nian's coming and indulgence, folks considered that night as a juncture of torture, which is called *Nian Guan* in Chinese, and they thought out a whole set of ways to get through that night. When the night came, every family made dinner early, extinguished fire and cleaned over, locked the door to all chicken pens and bullpens, sealed front and back doors of the house, and had Hogmanay dinner in the house. Since people didn't know what would happen after this dinner, it was extremely sumptuous. Not only that every family member had to dine together around a table to show harmony and reunion, but that before dinner, they had to pay respect to ancestors for their blessing to help them get through the night. After dinner, no one dared sleep but all huddled together and chatted to earn courage. This gradually comes to be the custom of staying up on New Year's Eve.

This custom first caught on in Southern and Northern dynasties. Many scholars in the period of Liang (502-557) wrote poems and articles about it. People lit candles or oil lamps to stay up all night, symbolizing that the light shone on all evils, plagues, and diseases and drove them away, and anticipated good luck and fortune in the new year. This custom has been handed down to the present.

When the clock strikes twelve at midnight of New Year's Eve, people will **eat *jiaozi*** (Chinese dumpling). In ancient time midnight was called *Zi Shi* and *Zi Shi* of New Year's Eve was the time when new year replaces old year. People eat *jiaozi* at this time because it means new replacing old and changing of year (which sounds similar to *jiaozi* in Chinese). That's how the name *jiaozi* came into being. It is also because that *jiaozi* made of flour are shaped like silver ingot, and plates of them being taking onto table implies the good wish of "making big fortune in the new and gold ingots keep running in," this custom of eating *jiaozi* has been kept till now.

Children especially like spending Spring Festival because they can get money on New Year's Eve, which is called **Ya Sui money** (given to children by elders). *Ya Sui* money is a new year given with good wishes. The money should be daintily put in a red paper bag and will be distributed to minor juniors by the elders after Hogmanay dinner or after the clock striking twelve at midnight. It is said that since year and the name of evil spirit sound the same (both are *Sui* in Chinese), *Ya Sui* money can keep evils away from juniors and ensure them a peaceful and healthy New Year.

After New Year's Eve it is the first day of lunar new year. From that day on, people begin visiting relatives and friends, paying New Year visit to each other. **Bai Nian** (Chinese for making New Year visit) is an important custom of Spring Festival and is a way of ridding the old, welcoming the new, and expressing good will to each other. On the one hand, it is out of respect for the elders and love for relatives and friends, and on the other hand, it is an activity for communication and deepening friendship. On these visits, people say something auspicious for happiness and health, wishing each other all the best in the new year.

During Spring Festival people also have the custom of **Tie Chunlian** (sticking New Year couplets). The original form of New Year couplets is so-called *Tao Fu* (peach wood charm). They first appeared in Zhou Dynasty (1046-256 BC) in the form of rectangular peach woods hanging at each side of door. In ancient Chinese myth, there is said to be a world of ghosts, in which is a mountain where grows a huge peach tree covering 3,000 *li* of areas. On the treetop there is a gold rooster. Every morning when the gold rooster crows ghosts that have wandered away at night will come back to this world. The gate of this world is in the northeast of the peach tree. Two god men stand at each side of the gate. If the ghosts do something cruel in the night, they will discover it immediately and catch the ghost, bind it with ropes made of reeds, and send it to feed tigers. Consequently all ghosts in that world fear those two god men. As a result, common people carve peach wood into their shapes and place them in front of their door to keep away evil and injury. Later, people simply carve the two god men's names on peach wood, believing that can also suppress evil and keep away vice. These peach woods are later called "peach wood charm."

When it came to Song Dynasty, people started writing

The custom of sticking couplets still prevails today. Photo by Chen Tingyou.

Temple fair of Changdian in Beijing.

couplets on peach wood, which serves three purposes. First, it still has the function of peach wood suppressing evil. Second, it expresses one's good wish. Third, it can be used as decoration to add beauty. Later couplets were written on red paper which symbolized happiness and fortune. They were to be stuck on both side of doors and windows to show people's wish for fortune and luck in the oncoming year. Because of strong advocacy of all dynasties, New Year couplets have become a special form of folk art in China, receiving long and high popularity.

To wish for the whole family's fortune, longevity, health and peace, people in some places still keep the custom of **sticking door god**. It is said that with two door gods stuck on the door, all sorts of demons and ghosts will be awed and turn away. For common people, door gods are tokens of righteousness and force. Ancient people believe that people with ugly faces usually are possessed with magic power and unnatural ability. They are just and kind and defeating ghosts and demons is their nature and responsibility. Zhong Kui, the ghost-catching master who is admired by all, is with such a strange shape and ugly face. Therefore door gods used by common people always have angry staring eyes and savage faces with various traditional weapons in hand, always ready to fight with ghosts that dare to challenge. Since door of common Chinese house have two pieces, usually door gods appear in pairs.

Cracker playing is children's favorite activity during Spring Festival. Legend has it that setting off crackers can drive away

"Baozhu Shenghua (Crackers Bring Flowers)" by Wu Youru, late-Qing Dynasty.

Annual Spring Festival Evening Party on TV becomes the focus of attention during the festival. Provided by Qin Xinmin.

goblins and expel demons, so every year from New Year's Eve, the sound of crackers exploding lasts a long while. The beautiful fireworks and sound of crackers add fun to the festive liveliness, being a unique sight during that time.

During Spring Festival, each region has its local traditional entertainments, with lion dance, dragon light dance, land boat rowing, and high tilt playing as the most common. Many regions hold temple fair, which is a tradition way to celebrate Spring Festival. It generally lasts from the first to the seventh of the first lunar month. In temple fair there is wonderful performance of lion dance and dragon dance and various kinds of handicrafts and local small eatings, which attract thousands and thousands of people celebrating the festival.

With the development of time, customs of spending Spring Festival have seen some changes too. For example, many cities have forbidden the playing of fireworks and crackers in case they cause fire or pollute environment. But this does not dampen the festive boisterousness. On New Year's Eve, family are still

getting together and having Hogmanay dinner while watching brilliant Spring Festival party until early morning of the first day of the first lunar month. In the heart of all descendents of Chinese nation, Spring Festival is always the most important.

Yuanxiao Festival

Name : *Yuanxiao* Festival (Lantern Festival)
Date: the 15th day of the first lunar month

The 15th day of the first lunar month is the traditional Chinese *Yuanxiao* Festival. Because the first lunar month is also called *"yuan"* month; the night of the 15th day of *yuan* month is the first night that the moon gets full; *xiao* means "night," so the festival is named *Yuanxiao* Festival or *Shangyuan* Festival, *Yuanxi* Festival or Lantern Festival.

The Chinese people have a custom of **enjoying lanterns** on Lantern Festival, which is said as "holding ceremonies of festival lanterns on the 15th day of the first lunar month." The custom come from the Taoist "Theory of Three Yuan": the 15th day of the first lunar month is *Shangyuan* Festival; that of the seventh lunar month is *Zhongyuan* Festival; and that of the tenth lunar month is *Xiayuan* Festival. These three *yuan* are in the charge of three officials: heaven, earth and human world respectively. The official of heaven likes joyful things, so lanterns should be lit on *Shangyuan* Festival. The custom of lighting lanterns on Lantern Festival has already appeared in the Han Dynasty. After generations of development, more and more varieties of lanterns come into being and the forms of playing vary too, for example, there are mirror-like lanterns, phoenix lanterns, colored glaze lanterns, and so on. Apart from lighting lanterns, people also set off fireworks to go with the festival atmosphere. That "Shining trees and sparkling fireworks weaves an unsleeping night" is the description of the beautiful scenes on the night of Lantern Festival.

The game of **guessing lantern riddles** is also a must on the Lantern Festival. Lantern riddles are a peculiar game of the

Chinese characters. The answer of a riddle is hidden behind a beautiful poem or some common sayings which are written on the paper sticked on the festival lanterns, and the visitors of the lanterns should try to find out it. It is similar to the "crosswords." The game of guessing lantern riddles first appears in the Song Dynasty. In the capital Lin'an (now Hangzhou) of the Southern Song Dynasty (1127-1279), there would be a lot of people setting and guessing lantern riddles on every occasion of Lantern Festival. Since riddles can give people both knowledge and happiness, they are thus welcomed by all classes of the society while spreading.

Eating rice glue balls is a characteristic custom of Lantern Festival. It is said that this custom originated in the Spring and Autumn Period (770-476 BC). The rice glue ball is also called *"tangyuan"* or *"yuanzi,"* which is a small ball made of glutinous rice with or without stuffing (usually sugar, bean paste, hawthorn or other fried fruits). It can be boiled, fried and steamed, and each means making it tasty. The Chinese people want everything to have a happy ending, so eating glue rice balls on the night when the moon gets full for the first time in a year indicates people's wish for a happy reunion and a peaceful life.

As the time goes by, more and more activities are added on the Lantern Festival. In cities there are lanterns ceremonies in which all patterns of lanterns are exhibited, and in the

*"Celebrating the Lantern Festival,"
New Year poster, Qing Dynasty.*

Taking joy in watching lanterns on the Lantern Festival on the 15th of the first lunar month.

countryside there are activities like setting off fireworks and walking on stilts. In some places there also develops some other activities such as playing the cloth lions, rowing boats on land, doing the *yangge* dance, playing the swings and playing *taiping* drums.

A father and his son are guessing the lantern riddle in the stream of people.

Spring Dragon Festival

Name: Spring Dragon Festival (the dragon lifts its head on the second day of the second lunar month)
Date: the second day of the second lunar month

The folklore goes that every second day of the second lunar month is the time when the dragon in charge of the rain lifts its head. From that day on rainfall will increase gradually, so it is called the "Spring Dragon Festival" or "Dragon Head Festival." There is a saying widely spread in the north of China that "the dragon lifts its head on the second day of the second lunar month and large barns will be full and small ones will overflow."

On every occasion of the Spring Dragon Festival, families in most of the areas in northern China will go to wells or rivers to fetch water with their lanterns on in the morning. Then they will come back home and turn on the light, burn joss sticks and offer up sacrifices. This ceremony was called "attracting the dragon in the field" in the old times. On this festival, every family should **eat noodles**, which means "lifting the dragon's head"; **fry cakes**, which means "eating the dragon's gallbladder" (the Chinese people believe that it is the gallbladder that decide one's courage); and **pop corn** so that "golden beans can blossom; dragon god can return to heaven and distribute the rain to the earth and crops can grow well."

A story about the origin of the Spring Dragon Festival prevails among people. In the Tang Dynasty, Wu Zetian the queen came to power and became the empress, which irritated Yuhuang Dadi in the heaven. He ordered the four dragon gods who are in charge of the rain not to rain a single drop in three years. However, the dragon god who is in charge of the heaven river couldn't bear to see people on earth being driven to death, so he broke Yuhuang Dadi's rule and secretly rained once. Yuhuang Dadi became so angry that he kept the dragon god under the mountain as a kind of torture, and a stele on the mountain read as follows:

The dragon king violates the heavenly rules by dropping rain
And is subject to thousands of years of punishment on earth
If ever he wishes to go back to the heavenly palace
It's only when golden beans give birth to flowers.

To save the kind-hearted dragon god, people went everywhere to find the golden beans. On the second day of the second lunar month the next year, people found the secret of golden beans when they were tedding the seeds of corn: since the corn is just like golden beans, isn't that the golden beans blossom when the corn is popped? So every family began to pop the corn and set up the altar to offer the blossomed "golden beans" as sacrifices. The dragon god lifted his head and saw all this. Knowing that people are trying to rescue him, he cried to Yuhuang Dadi, "The golden beans have blossomed, so please set me free!" Yuhuang Dadi had no choice but to call the dragon god back to heaven and give back his job. From then on it became a habit that people pop corn on the second day of the second lunar month.

Actually, it is just the characteristic of North China Monsoon that the rainfalls begin to grow after the second day of the second

"The Dragon Lifts Its Head on the Second Day of the Second Lunar Month," New Year Poster.

lunar month. However, seen from another perspective, the festival also shows people's wishes for fine weather and a better harvest.

Pure Brightness Festival

Name: Pure Brightness Festival (Tomb-Sweeping Day)
Date: the seasonal division point Pure Brightness (Apr. 5th or 6th)

Pure Brightness Festival is a very peculiar one among all the traditional Chinese festivals which are still popular today. It is a great festival as well as an important seasonal division point. 107 days later than the Beginning of Winter, 15 days than the Spring Solstice and around April 5th, it plays a special role in the alternation of seasons. To learn the beginning of Pure Brightness Festival, we have to first know about a festival which was very famous in the past but has lost its popularity today – *Hanshi* Festival. *Hanshi* Festival is one or two days before the Pure Brightness Festival, and it is also called "Cold Festival" or "Smoking-Banning Festival." This day was believed as a kind of commemoration of a loyal court official in the Spring and Autumn Period – Jie Zitui.

Jie Zitui was a capable minister in the state of Jin, the prince of which was Chong Er. A civil war broke out in Jin and Prince Chong Er had to escape abroad. During the exile of about nineteen years, Jie Zitui had always been by the prince's side in spite of all the difficulties. He had even made broth out of the flesh on his leg to feed the prince when they were short of food. Later when Chong Er became the king, which is known as Jin Wengong (Wen Duke of Jin) in history, he handsomely rewarded those who accompanied him in hardship, leaving only Jie Zitui neglected. Many people felt very indignant to Prince Chong Er for Jie Zitui and advised Jie to ask for reward from the duke. But Jie despised those people who struggled for rewards so much that he packed his luggage and retired into Mian Moutain with his mother.

When Jin Wengong got the news, he felt so ashamed that he

29

took some people and went to the mountain to find Jie Zitui. However, the bumpiness of the mountain road and the thickness of the forest added great difficulty to the searching of only two people. Someone suggested that they could set fire to the forest so that Jie would be forced out. Wengong took this advice and the fire thus seared its way all over the mountain. Nonetheless, Jie Zitui still didn't show up. When the fire was out, people found that Jie had already died under a willow with his mother on the back. What's more, a letter written in blood was found from the hole of the tree. It said:

> *Giving meat and heart to my lord,*
> *Hoping my lord will always be upright.*
> *An invisible ghost under a willow*
> *Is better than a loyal minister beside my lord.*
> *If my lord has a place in his heart for me,*

Sweeping tomb on the Pure Brightness Day.

Please make self-reflection when remembering me.
I have a clear conscience in the nether world,
Being pure and bright in my offices year after year.

To commemorate Jie Zitui's exhortation with death, Jin Wengong decided this day to be the *Hanshi* Festival and ordered that no fire should be permitted in the whole country on that day. The next year when Wengong went to hold a memorial ceremony on that mountain with other ministers, they found the willow shooting again. So they named the willow "Pure Bright Willow" and christened the day after *Hanshi* Festival "Pure Brightness Festival."

It is usually bright and clean on the Pure Brightness Day, people often go to **sweep the tombs** of their relatives, offer sacrifices to their ancestors, **go for a walk in the countryside** and **plant willows** on this day.

The Chinese people have traditional respect to the seniors, especially to their forefathers that have passed away. Therefore every time when it comes to the Pure Brightness Festival, the families will pay a solemn visit to the tombs of their forefathers. They remove the weed around the tombs, add some new earth to them, burn joss sticks and put some food and paper money there to show their sincere affection and respect to the dead. This is called *"shangfen"* or "sweeping the tombs." However, as cremation is gradually taking the place of ground burying, it is

On the Pure Brightness Festival, students go to the martyrs' park and mourn for them.

"Flying Kites in the Spring Wind," New Year poster.

harder to see tombs in the fields nowadays. But still people can commemorate their forefathers in other ways or they can go to the martyrs' park and mourn for them by offering flowers and wreaths onto their tombs.

At the time of Pure Brightness Festival, the weather is becoming warmer and warmer; trees and grass began to shoot up; the open country is flooded with vigorous greenness – it's just the right time for people to go outside and relax themselves. They often go to the countryside with their friends to breathe the fresh air and indulge themselves in the blue sky, green trees, viridescent grass and beautiful flowers. The ancient people called the custom of walking in the countryside "*Taqing,*" so Pure Brightness Festival is also known as "*Taqing* Festival." People also wear a willow twig on head to expel ghosts and disasters and pray for peace and happiness. There was also a custom of "picking shepherd's purse while walking in the countryside," and it can still be seen today. Around the time of Pure Brightness Festival, girls and women will pick some fresh potherb and make dumplings of them. Some women also like to wear the flower of shepherd's purse in their hair.

There are also customs of flying kites, playing tug-of-war and playing swings on the Pure Brightness Festival. It is golden time to sow then, so a lot of agricultural proverbs are about Pure

Brightness Festival and agricultural activities, for example, "Plant melons and beans around Pure Brightness Festival." In the ancient time people also planted willows on this festival, just as the ancient poem goes, "A street of willows covered with a green veil, weaves the Pure Brightness Day."

Dragon Boat Festival

Name: Dragon Boat Festival
Date: the fifth day of the fifth lunar month

About the origin of Dragon Boat Festival there are a lot of versions, the most influential one of which is that it is a festival that commemorates Qu Yuan. This version has almost been taken as a common sense among the Chinese people.

Qu Yuan (c.340-278 BC) was a *dafu* (senior state official in feudal China) in the state of Chu in the Warring States Period. Among the seven states then (Qi, Chu ,Yan, Han, Zhao, Wei and Qin), Qin was the most powerful one and it intended to conquer the other six and dominate the world. Qu's capability won the recognition of Chu Huaiwang (Huai King of Chu). However, Qu's opinion that Chu should carry out a political reform and cooperate with the other states to fight against Qin met opposition from his fellow officials. They spoke ill of Qu before Huaiwang, and as a result, Huaiwang gradually became estranged from Qu, and finally he drove Qu out of the capital of Chu. Finally, Chu was defeated by Qin. Grieved and indignant, Qu Yuan jumped into Miluo River and ended his life. That day was just the fifth day of the fifth lunar month in 278 BC.

When people got the news that Qu Yuan had drowned himself, they all got very sad and rowed to get his dead body but failed. To save the body from the fish, people threw food into the river to distract their attention. From then on, people always row dragon boats on rivers to mourn over Qu Yuan on the fifth day of the fifth lunar month every year. Moreover, they fill the bamboo cans with rice and throw them into rivers as a memorial ceremony. It was said that once someone met Qu Yuan

Portrait of Poet Qu Yuan.

33

by the river and Qu said, "The food you gave me has been robbed by the dragon. You'd better wrap the rice with bamboo or reed leaves and fasten it with colored threads, for these things are what dragons are most afraid of." Since then, people began to commemorate Qu Yuan with *zongzi* which are made of glutinous rice wrapped in bamboo or reed leaves, and thus *zongzi* become the traditional food of Dragon Boat Festival.

In this way, the tradition of eating *zongzi* and rowing dragon boats was handed down to the later generations.

The second legend of Dragon Boat Festival is related to a historical figure: Wu Zixu. Wu (?-484 BC) was from the state of Chu in the Warring States Period. With his father and brothers having been killed by the king of Chu, he sought refuge with the state of Wu and helped it fight all the way to the city of Ying, the capital of Chu. He dug out the dead body of the king of Chu from the tomb and whipped it three hundred times as a kind of revenge. Later the state of Wu got involved in a war with Yue. Wu Zixu advised the king of Wu not to compromise with Yue, but the king believed false accusations about Wu Zixu and granted him a sword to commit suicide. Wu said, "After my death, please dig out my eyes and hang them on the eastern door of the capital of Wu so that I can see how Yue's army march into Wu's land and conquer it." Then he killed himself. The King of Wu was irritated by these words. He issued an order to put Wu Zixu's body in a leather bag and threw it into the river on the fifth day of the fifth lunar month. Therefore Dragon Boat Festival is also considered as a commemoration of Wu Zixu.

A third version of the origin of Dragon Boat Festival is said to honor Cao E, a filial daughter in Eastern Han Dynasty (25-220). Cao's father got drowned in the river and the body could not be found for days. The only 14-year-old Cao E cried day and night by the river and finally jumped into it on the fifth day of the fifth lunar month. Five days later, she returned with her father's body. To commemorate Cao E's filial behavior, people built a "Cao E Temple" at the place where she jumped into the river. Apart from that, the village she lived was rechristened as "Cao E Village," and the river she jumped in was named "Cao E River."

Dragon Boat Festival has lasted for more than two thousand

Selling the Calamus.

Dragon-Boat racing in Hong Kong.

years in China. Generally speaking, the custom of celebrating is more or less the same over different areas, such as Dragon-Boat races, eating *zongzi*, wearing perfume sachets, and putting mugwort or calamus at home.

Dragon-Boat race is an aquatic athletic sport which has had a long history in China. In some areas it is called "rowing Dragon Boats" or "Dragon-Boat competition." The custom of Dragon-Boats competition on Dragon Boat Festival prevails in the southern part of the drainage of Yangtze River. In the 29th year of Qianlong's rule in the Qing Dynasty (1736), Taiwan started to hold Dragon-Boat competition, and Jiang Yuanjun, the magistrate of the Taiwan prefecture, then had once presided over a friendly contest. Nowadays there are Dragon-Boat races in Taiwan and Hong Kong on the fifth day of the fifth lunar month every year. Besides, Dragon Boats have also found their ways to foreign lands like Japan and Korea. In the year of 1980, Dragon-Boat race was taken into the list of the Chinese national sports events. The "Qu Yuan Cup" Dragon-Boat race is being held every year. On June 16th in 1991 (the fifth day of the fifth lunar month), the first international Dragon-Boat race Festival was hold in the second hometown of Qu Yuan: the city of Yueyang, Hunan Province. Before the competition there was a "Dragon-Head ceremony" which have both kept the essence of traditional ceremony and also added some elements of the modern time.

35

The dragonhead was carried into the ancestral temple of Qu Yuan and was "*shanghong*"(was draped a length of red cloth) by the sports man. Then the host delivered a funeral oration and "*kaiguang*"(drew the eyes) on the dragonhead. After that all of the attendants bowed three times to the dragonhead, and then it was finally carried to Miluo River – the competition site. Over 600,000 people attended the competition, trade fair and party, which makes it an unprecedented grand occasion.

Eating *zongzi* on Dragon Boat Festival is another important tradition among Chinese people. *Zongzi* has had a long history and it has developed a lot of types. It is recorded that early in the Spring-Autumn Period *zongzi* had appeared in an embryonic form as "horn millet," which was the millet wrapped by the leaves of wildrice, and "bamboo-canned *zong*," which was the rice cooked in a sealed bamboo can.

In the Jin Dynasty (265-420), *zongzi* was officially accepted as the food eaten on Dragon Boat Festival. Then in the North and South dynasties there appeared mixed *zongzi* in which the rice was stuffed with meat, chestnuts, jujube, red beans and so on. Moreover, *zongzi* could also be given to relatives and friends as presents. In the Tang Dynasty the rice used to make *zongzi* had been "as white as the jade," and conic-shaped and diamond-shaped *zongzi* began to show up. The word of "*Datang zongzi*" (*zongzi* in the Tang imperial) even appeared in some Japanese literature. In the Song Dynasty "*Mijian zong*" (*zongzi* with glazed fruit in) appeared. The poet Su Dongpo (1037-1101) also wrote about *zongzi* in his poems that "In *zongzi* I can always see waxberries"). In the period of Yuan (1206-1368) and Ming dynasties, the leaves with which *zongzi* are wrapped changed from wildrice to bamboo leaves, and later the reed leaves were also put into use. The varieties of supplementary materials also increased, for example, bean paste, pork, pine nuts, jujubes and walnuts had already appeared.

(Top) Zongzi *(glutinous rice cake with meat stuffing).*
(Bottom) *Reed leaves used to wrap* zongzi.

Even by now, the Chinese families are still soaking glutinous rice, washing the bamboo or reed leaves and making *zongzi* whenever the fifth lunar month approaches. Moreover, more varieties of *zongzi* are developed. Judging from the stuffing, the jujube-stuffed *zongzi* in Beijing plays a main role in the North,

Various sachets.

while stuffing like bean past, rice, ham, and yolk are common in the South, in which *zongzi* in Zhejiang Province is the most typical one. The custom of eating *zongzi* has been popular in China for thousands of years. It even crossed the border and spread to Korea, Japan and the counties in Southeast Asia.

The saying goes that "wearing willows on Pure Bright Festival while keeping *aicao* (mugwort) on Dragon Boat Festival." People believe that the fifth lunar month is deleterious, so **putting some mugwort and calamus at home** is regarded as an important activity on Dragon Boat Festival. Every family will clean their doors and put the mugwort and calamus on the lintel or hang them in the ceilings to expel the evil spirit and prevent diseases. *Aicao* is also called *jia'ai, aihao*. Its stalk and leaves contain a kind of volatilizable aromadendrin, the special aroma of which can drive off insects and keep the air crisp. The calamus is a kind of perennial water herbage. Its long and narrow leaves also contain a kind of volatilizable aromadendrin which can make people refreshed, can do good to their bones and kill insects. Seen in this way, there are actually some elements of truth for the ancient people to keep mugwort and calamus at home, and thus Dragon

37

Chinese Festivals

Boat Festival is also known as the "Health Festival."

Hanging Zhong Kui's picture to scare off ghost is also a special custom of Dragon Boat Festival. In the drainage of Yangtze River and Huai River, people all hang the picture of Zhong Kui to guard their family from ghosts. The story of Zhong Kui goes like this: Tang Xuanzong (an emperor of the Tang Dynasty, 685-762) was suffering from a plague. One day he dreamed of two ghosts chasing each other in the imperial court. The younger ghost that was in red stole Concubine Yang's sachet and the emperor's flute and ran around the imperial court. The elder one that wore a gown and a cap, however, caught the younger one, dug out his eyes and swallow them down. Xuanzong cried out and the elder ghost said, "My name is Zhong Kui. I failed in the imperial examination, but I'd like to help your majesty get rid of ghosts." When the king woke up, he recovered instantly. Afterwards he asked Wu Daozi the painter to draw a picture of Zhong Kui based on his dream. Then he issued an order that the picture should be hung on the Dragon Boat Festival to guard against ghosts.

The custom of **drinking realgar liquor** is very popular among people in the drainage of Yangtze River. Realgar liquor is a kind of liquor with realgar in it, and realgar is a kind of mineral containing sulfide which can keep the vipers and insects off. "The Story of a White Snake" which is still well-known today has a scene that the human-shaped White Snake return to her original form after drinking the realgar liquor. Thus people believed that the poisonous insects such as snakes, scorpions and centipedes can be scared off by the realgar liquor, and drinking realgar liquor can prevent them from the deleterious stuff and keep them healthy.

There is also a custom of **wearing sachets** on Dragon Boat Festival. The sachets are said to indicate preventing evils but are actually a kind of decoration on the clothes. In the sachets there are usually vermillion, realgar, and some aromatic substances. Wrapped in the silk, these fragrant stuffs give out spells of faint scent. You can tie all shapes of sachets into a string with colorful threads. It will be very pretty.

Up to now, Dragon Boat Festival has developed into a very

"Zhong Kui ," New Year poster.

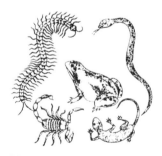

Five poisonous things (snake, scorpion, toad, gecko and centipede).

popular and grand festival in China, and the ancient stories and legends has given it remarkable vitality that can last for ages.

Double Seventh Festival

Name: Double Seventh Festival (the Praying-for-Cleverness Ceremony)

Date: the seventh day of the seventh lunar month

The seventh day of the seventh lunar month is the Double Seventh Festival in China. The folklore goes that it is the day when Herd-boy and Weaving-girl reunite with each other. The beautiful love story about the origin of this festival is still popular today.

It is said that a long time ago, a clever and honest man named Niu Lang (Herd-boy) was living in the Niu village at the west of Nanyang city. Niu Lang's parents died when he was very young and he had to live with his brother and sister-in-law. The latter was very cruel and mean to Niu and always forced him to do some hard work. Finally she even drove Niu out of her family. Poor Niu only had an old cow with him. One day the old cow suddenly told Niu, "Tomorrow is the seventh day of the seventh lunar month; the seven daughters of Yuhuang Dadi will come to earth and have a bathe. The youngest one that named Zhi Nü (Weaving-girl) is the cleverest. Hide her clothes and she will be your wife." Niu Lang was aroused by what the cow had said and decided to have a try.

"Herd-boy and Weaving-girl" by
Lu Youru, late-Qing Dynasty.

When it came to that day, Niu Lang hided himself in the reed by the river beforehand. Soon seven fairies descended from the heaven. They took off their clothes and jumped into the river. Right then Niu Lang bounced up from the reed, grabbed Zhi Nü's clothes and dashed backwards immediately. This had terrified the seven fairies and the six of them flew to the heaven with their clothes on, leaving only the youngest Zhi Nü startled in the river. Niu Lang stumbled that he would return the clothes as long as she promised to marry him. Zhi Nü found that Niu Lang was the kind of man that she loved, so she nodded bashfully. After the marriage Herd-boy and Weaving-girl lead a happy life and they loved each other very much. Later they gave birth to a son and a daughter. How perfect the life was! However, the Queen Mother of the Western Heavens was irritated by their behavior and forced Zhi Nü to return to the heaven.

Niu Lang put on his cowhide shoes and brought his kids with him to chase Zhi Nü back. When it came to the edge of success, the Queen Mother of the Western heavens pulled out a hairpin from her hair. With just one wave of the hairpin, she brought about a billowing river, which separated the two lovers at each bank. They could do nothing but weep with each other. Fortunately, the magpies were moved by their sincere love. That's said to be the origin of the Milky Way, Altair and Vega. Hundreds of thousands of them flew there and they formed a magpie bridge so that Herd-boy and Weaving-girl can get together again on the bridge. Not being able to make any change to this, the Queen Mother of the Western Heavens had to permit them to reunite

"Threading the Needles" by Wu Youru, late-Qing Dynasty.

with each other every seventh day of the seventh lunar month.

From then on, whenever it comes to that day, young girls will dress themselves in new clothes and tried to find the Herd-boy and the Weaving-girl stars in the sky at night, expecting to see their yearly reunion and praying to gods that they can be as intelligent and talented as Zhi Nü and can have a happy marriage. That's how the Praying-for-Cleverness Ceremony originated.

American couple spending a Chinese-style Valentine's Day.

The Praying-for-Cleverness Ceremony is a very exciting day in the Chinese countryside. Young girls wear new clothes, worship the two stars and **"pray to Zhi Nü for cleverness"**. There are many kinds of prays, the most common one of which is the pray for the talent of threading needles. Young women bring out colorful threads and seven needles. The girl who can pull a thread through these needles will be regarded as "talented lady."

The Double Seventh Festival is considered as the Chinese Valentine's Day. The story that Herd-boy and Weaving-girl reunited on the Magpie Bridge casts a romantic light on this festival. It is said that you can even hear the sweet whispers between these two lovers if you sit under the grape vine on that day.

Ullam-bana Festival

Name: Ullam-bana Festival (Ghosts' Festival or *Zhongyuan* Festival)
Date: the 15th day of the seventh lunar month

The 15th day of the seventh lunar month every year is "Ullam-bana Festival" or "*Zhongyuan* Festival," and in some places it is also called "Ghosts' Festival" or "*Shigu*." It is a festival from Buddhism and also a day to offer sacrifices to the ancestors. People believe that the hell is governed by Diguan Dadi. Every year on his birthday, which is the 15th day of the seventh lunar month, he will open the door of hell and all the ghosts will come to earth. Then people will be able to provide food and drink for them as a kind of comfort.

Ullam-bana comes from Sanskrit. It originated from a Buddhist ritual and means "to rescue the inversely hung." It is said that a disciple of Sakyamuni saw his mother being hung inversely in the hell and he thus asked the Buddha to release her soul from purgatory. Sakyamuni told him to prepare a hundred kinds of food for all the Buddhist monks in that area on the 15th day of the seventh lunar month so that his mother will get released. This is the beginning of "Ullam-bana Festival."

People began to follow this custom from the Liang Dynasty in the South and North Period and it gradually became the "*Zhongyuan* Festival." Later apart from providing food for the monks, activities like "*baichan*" and "*fangyankou*" are added into the customs. When it comes to the day, the seat of *fashi* (the person who carry out the ritual, usually a Buddhist) and the *shigu* platform will be prepared beforehand at the door of the village. Before the seat of *fashi* is the Kitigarbha Bodhisattva whose job is to release the souls of the ghosts in hell from purgatory, and dishes of flour peach and rice are laid below. Three memorial tablets and an evocating flag are standing on the *shigu* platform. When it comes to the afternoon, every family will put the cooked pig, sheep, chicken and duck and all kinds of cakes and fruits onto the *shigu* platform. The leader will stick a triangle paper flag of different colors in each offering, and the paper may read "grand ritual of Ullam-bana" or "the door of hell is open," and so on. The ceremony starts in a piece of grand and solemn religious music. Then the *fashi* takes the lead to strike the *muyu* (a wooden stuff stroke by monks when chanting sutras) and chant incantation. After that flour peaches and rice are scattered in all directions for three times. This ceremony is called "**Fangyankou**."

When the night descends, every family will burn incense to the Buddha on the floor in front of the door. The more, the better. It is called "**butian**," which indicates that the crops will grow well.

"**Drifting river lanterns**" is also necessary on *Zhongyuan* Festival. A "river lantern" (water lantern) is a lantern fixed on a small board. They are often made of colorful papers and are usually shaped as lotuses. These lanterns will be lit up and placed onto the river. "Drifting river lanterns" first started from monasteries and then got popular among common people. According to the traditional point of view, river lanterns are drifted to guide the spirit of those who died unjustly. When the lantern goes out, the mission of guiding the spirit across *Naihe*

Folk artist drawing facial make-up for folk play "Mu Lian rescuing his mother".

Drifting river lanterns on Ullam-bana Festival in the ancient town of Shanghai.

Bridge (the bridge which the dead people should cross in the Buddhist legend) is done. People believe that *Zhongyuan* Festival is a festival of ghosts, so it is also necessary to put on lanterns and celebrate for them. But since ghosts are different from people, the lanterns in *Zhongyuan* Festival should also be different from those in *Shangyuan* Festival (Lantern Festival). As a result, lanterns in *Shangyuan* are lit on the land, while lanterns in *Zhongyuan* are lit on the river. All the shops will also be closed to give way to the ghosts. In the middle of every street there will be a table to place fresh fruits and "ghosts' bread" every hundred paces, with Taoists singing some "songs for ghosts" which people can barely understand. This ceremony is called "*Shiger*."

Nowadays, this festival isn't very popular among people and just appears in some grand ceremonies in monasteries. Instead, it developed a lot after spreading to Japan and has become a great activity which is only second to the New Year Festival in Japan.

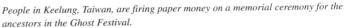

People in Keelung, Taiwan, are firing paper money on a memorial ceremony for the ancestors in the Ghost Festival.

Mid-Autumn Festival

Name: Mid-Autumn Festival

Date: the 15th day of the eighth lunar month

According to the Chinese lunar calendar, the seventh, eighth and ninth lunar months comprise autumn. The eighth lunar month is in the middle of autumn, and the 15th of the eighth month is in the middle of this month, so the festival is called "Mid-Autumn Festival." In autumns it is usually clear and cool and there are seldom wandering clouds in the sky, so the moon is particularly bright and clear at night. It is on the night of the 15th day in the eighth lunar month that the moon becomes full, so it is the golden time for people to enjoy the moon. The full moon is considered as a symbol of reunion. Therefore Mid-Autumn Festival is also called "the Reunion Festival," and it is a traditional festival only second to the Spring Festival.

The Mid-Autumn Festival has had a long history, and

The Mid-Autumn Festival Evening Party in 2005 of CCTV.

offering sacrifices to the moon and enjoy the moonlight were very important customs. There was an institutional convention among the ancient kings that they should offer sacrifices to the sun in spring and to the moon in autumn. This custom also existed among common people. As the time goes by, to enjoy the moon became more important, and the serious honoring ceremony turned into light-hearted entertainment. The custom of **enjoying the moon** on Mid-Autumn Festival was very popular in the Tang Dynasty. A lot of poems of some distinguished poets were odes about the moon. Activities concerning the moon became even more influential in Song, Ming and Qing dynasties. Up to the present time there are still many relics named "Praying-to-Moon Altar," "Praying-to-Moon Summerhouse," and "Observing Moon Tower." The "Moon Altar" in Beijing was built for the royal families to offer sacrifices to the moon in the period of Jiajing in Ming Dynasty. Nowadays the custom of offering sacrifices to the moon is replaced by the large-scaled and colorful activities of enjoying oneself with families and friends.

Moon Cakes.

Like eating *zongzi* on Dragon Boat Festival and eating *tangyuan* on the Lantern Festival, **eating moon cakes** on Mid-Autumn Festival is a traditional Chinese custom. The moon cake is round, which signifies *"tuanyuan"*(reunion; in Chinese "round" is *"yuan"*), so it is also called *"tuanyuan* cake" in some places. Moon cakes are the essentials of Mid-Autumn Festival. Throughout the history the moon cake has always been seen as a symbol of good luck and happy reunion. On the occasion of every Mid-Autumn Festival, the whole family will get together, eating moon cakes, enjoying the bright moon and talking about everything they like. What a joyful scene it is!

The custom of eating moon cakes on Mid-Autumn Festival has had a long history in China. There are different versions about the origin of it, and one of them goes like this: When Li Shimin (or Tang Taizong, the Tang emperor, 566-635) was in power, General Li Jing (571-649) returned from his victory against Xiongnu (Hun, an ancient ethnic group in the north of China) on the 15th day of the eighth lunar month. At that time a businessman from Turpan (a place in northwestern China) offered some cakes to the king to celebrate the victory. Taizong took out the round cake and pointed to the moon with a smile, "I'd like to invite the toad (in the Chinese culture toad stands for moon) to enjoy the *Hu* cake (cake from "Hu" people, the way that people of the Han nationality called those of the ethnic groups in ancient China)." Then he shared the cakes with the ministers. Since then the custom of eating *Hu* cakes began to spread all over the country. There is also a legend that the later emperor Xuanzong had once enjoyed the moon and eaten *Hu* cakes with his favorite Concubine Yang (719-756). Li didn't like the name of "*Hu* cake," so Concubine Yang looked at the moon and said casually, "Why not moon cake?" In this way the name of "moon cake" was finally settled.

There are many types of moon cakes in China, and the recipes as well as flavors vary in different areas. It can mainly be divided into five types according to the producing areas: Beijing, Tianjin, Guangzhou, Suzhou, and Chaozhou. Each has its strong point. The stuffing of moon cakes is either sugary or salt; either meat or fruits. There are also some flower patterns and characters on the moon cakes, which makes them not only tasteful but also beautiful.

The poem "In the Still of the Night" written by the great poet Li Bai (701-762) in Tang Dynasty is so famous among the Chinese people that even a little child can recite it:

I descry bright moonlight in front of my bed.
I suspect it to be hoary frost on the floor.
I watch the bright moon, as I tilt back my head.
I yearn, while stooping, for my homeland more.

The poem showed the exact feelings of those who are far away from their homes on Mid-Autumn Festival. They are not able to

"Chang E" by Wu Youru, late-Qing Dynasty.

return to their homes and cannot spend the holiday with their families, so they can only enjoy the bright moon which symbols happiness and reunion and repose their good wishes in the moonlight.

Ever since ancient China, there have been a lot of legends and stories about the moon, the most famous of which is "Chang E's flight to the moon." Chang E was the wife of Hou Yi, the hero who shot down nine suns in the ancient Chinese legend. It is said that she ate the elixir of life given by the Queen Mother of the Western Heavens without her husband's permission. Thus she turned into a goddess and flew to the moon. A second legend is the story of "Wu Gang cutting the laurel." Wu Gang was a person just like Sisyphus. He sought immortality and became a god, but was exiled to the moon for some mistake and was ordered to cut the laurel in front of the "*Guanghan* Palace" (the palace on the moon in the legend) every day. The laurel was of over five hundred *zhang* (a unit of length equal to 3.3333 meters), and whenever Wu managed to cut a slash on the tree, it will heal instantly. So he had to repeat the hard work forever in vain. It is said that if you observe carefully, you can even see the Jade hare and toad on the moon on Mid-Autumn Festival. All these legends have tinted the moon with some mysterious and romantic colors, and the children today also like to hear these stories from their parents when enjoying the moon.

Double Ninth Festival

Name: Double Ninth Festival
Date: the ninth day of the ninth lunar month

The ninth day of the ninth lunar month is the "Double Ninth Festival" in China. In the ancient Chinese book "*Yijing* (or *I-Ching, The Book of Changs*)," "six" was seen as the *yin* number, while "nine" the *yang* number. The ninth day of the ninth lunar month include two *yang* numbers, so the day is called "Double *Yang*" or "Double Nine." The earliest record of the name of "Double Ninth Festival" was in the period of Three Kingdoms (220-280).

The origin of Double Ninth Festival can date back to at least the beginning of Han Dynasty. At that time, Queen Lü was so jealous of Concubine Qi, who is one of the favorite of Liu Bang (the first emperor of the Han Dynasty, 256 or 247-195 BC), that she ill-treated the latter and drove her maid out of the imperial palace to marry a common people. This maid, who is known as Miss Jia, told people that in the imperial palace, every ninth day of the ninth lunar month, they wear dogwoods and drink chrysanthemum wine, otherwise there would be disasters. Later many common people followed the custom and it gradually prevailed all over the country.

"*Tao Yuanming Enjoying Chrysanthemums*" *by Jiang Zhaohe.*

The custom of **wearing dogwoods** was already very popular in the Tang Dynasty. The dogwood is heavy-scented plant whose fruit is edible and stock and leaves can be medicinal materials. They can expel insects, get rid of the humidity, help digestion and cure inner heat. The ancient people believed that planting dogwoods on Double Ninth Festival could prevent diseases and avoid disasters. They also wear the dogwoods on arms or heads or put them in sachets. Most of people that follow the custom are women and children, and in some places men also wear them.

Besides dogwoods, chrysanthemums are also worn by people

Aged people are enjoying chrysanthemums in a park on Double Ninth Festival.

on Double Ninth Festival. Chrysanthemums blossom in the ninth lunar month and they have a beautiful name of "flower of longevity." The custom of **wearing chrysanthemums** appeared in the Tang Dynasty already and was always very popular throughout the time afterwards. When it came to the Qing Dynasty, people in Beijing began to stick the chrysanthemums on doors and windows to "get rid of the bad luck and bring in the good ones," which is an alteration of the custom of wearing Chrysanthemums on head.

It is always bright and clear around Double Ninth Festival and the chrysanthemums are blossoming then, so drinking wine while enjoying chrysanthemums is also one if the traditional customs in this festival. Enjoying chrysanthemums and drinking chrysanthemum wine originated from the Eastern Jin Dynasty (317-420) in which the great poet Tao Yuanming (365-427) lived. Tao was famous for his reclusive life in the countryside, his excellence in poetry, and his favor of wine and also chrysanthemums. Other people imitated him and this custom of enjoying chrysanthemums thus came into being. The scholar officials then added feasting to go with enjoying chrysanthemums in order to be more like Tao Yuanming. This custom spread widely in the capital Kaifeng in the Song Dynasty. After the Qing Dynasty, with the time not limited to the ninth day of the ninth lunar month, this custom became even more popular. But the grandest celebrations, of course, were still around the Double Ninth Festival. Crisp air, clear sky, blossoming chrysanthemums all over the fields – it is really a joyful life!

There is also a custom of **eating "Double Ninth cakes"** on the festival later. The Double Ninth cake is a kind of food made of flour. It can

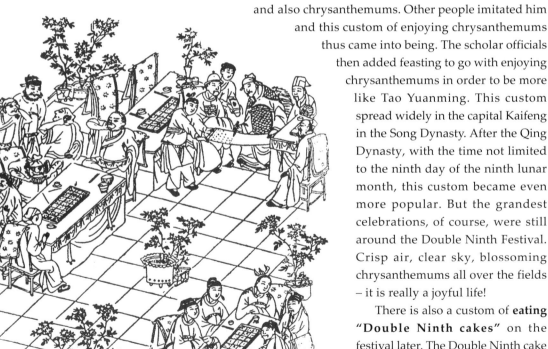

Chrysanthemum Party.

be added jujubes, gingkoes apricots, and pine nuts to become sweet, or be added meat to become salt. Some special Double Ninth cakes should have nine layers and look like a tower. There should be two little sheep on the top, which is to go with the "double *yang*" (sheep in Chinese is "*yang*").

People also like to **climb mountains** on this festival, so Double Ninth Festival is also called "Mountain-climbing Festival." It is really refreshing to climb mountains and enjoy the beauty of nature at this bright and clear time in autumn. Climbing mountains on Double Ninth Festival was already prevailing in the Tang Dynasty, and a lot of poems were devoted to this custom, such as "On the Ninth Day of the Ninth Lunar Festival: Thinking of My Brothers in Shandong" written by the great poet Wang Wei (701-761) in the Tang Dynasty:

All alone in a foreign land,
I am twice as homesick on this day.
When brothers carry dogwood up the mountain,
Each of them a branch, and my branch missing.

Apart from expelling bad luck and disasters, climbing mountains also indicates "climbing to a higher position," and it is also an important reason why ancient people pay much attention about this custom. Another reason that climbing mountains are valued by people, especially by the elderly is that it has a meaning of "climb to a longevous life." Also for this reason people believe that climbing mountains can make people live a more longevous life.

There is no custom of planting dogwood on Double Ninth Festival nowadays, but many people still climb up the mountains and enjoy the chrysanthemums together with the beautiful scenery of autumn. In the recent years something new was added into the old festival and it became an annual "Respect-the-Senior Festival." Every time it comes to this day, people will hold all kinds of activities to show their wish for the senior people that they can always keep healthy and happy.

Dong Jie

Name: *Dong Jie* (Winter Solstice)

Date: the seasonal division point Winter Solstice (December 22nd or 23rd)

Winter Solstice, colloquially named *"Dong Jie,"* is a very important festival in ancient times. Winter Solstice comes fifteen days later than the Great Snow. With the daytime reaching its shortest time in the northern hemisphere on that day and the night becoming the longest, it is the coldest day in a year. It also suggests the arriving of spring and is the turning point between winter and spring. Thus among the twenty four seasonal divisions, Winter Solstice is the most important one.

The ancient people thought that when Winter Solstice came, though it was still cold, the spring was already around the corner. People who were still out should come back home to show that they had reached their destination at the end of a year. People in Fujian and Taiwan provinces regard Winter Solstice as the day of reunion of families; for it is a day when they offer sacrifices to their ancestors, and anyone that doesn't return home will be seen as a person who has forgotten his ancestors.

The night of Winter Solstice is the longest in a year, so a lot of families will take advantage of this night to **make "Winter Solstice dumplings"** of glutinous rice. To distinguish it from *"ci sui"*(bid farewell to the outgoing year) on the lunar New Year's Eve, the day before Winter Solstice is named *"tian sui"* or *"ya sui,"* suggesting that though a year (the Chinese *"sui"* means "year") hasn't ended, everybody has been a year older.

The traditional Chinese customs may differ from each other in some details, but they are more or less the same on the whole. When making Winter Solstice dumplings, people always knead the food into some little animals such as little cats, dogs, rabbits and tigers at the request of kids. Kids often get very happy on the occasion like this. Before eating the Winter Solstice dumplings, people should stick a dumpling behind doors, windows, tables, cabins, beds and lights. It is called "killing time," because dumplings in these places can only be baked after sending off the Kitchen God. It is said that if some woman in the family is pregnant then, she will give birth to a boy if the dumplings expand, other wise, it will be a girl. The number of people that eat Winter Solstice dumplings should be even so that it can be a good omen. At the end of the feast, if there are two dumplings left, the married people will get whatever they want in the future; while if there is only one left, the single ones will lead a life they wish. Some families also offer sacrifices to gods and their ancestors with some seasonable fruits and domestic animals. People may "**put the winter rice in sun**," too. That is to wash the rice with water, insolate them in the sun and finally put them away so that they can be made into porridge for the people who may get ill in the future.

"Alleviating the Coldness in 81days," New Year poster. After the Winter Solstice, people will welcome bright and beautiful spring through 81 cold days. Not only could this kind of poster be used as a calendar but also regarded as a beautiful adornment.

Statutory Festivals

Chinese statutory festivals and memorial days can be roughly divided into three types: the first type is those when all the citizens are entitled to a holiday, including New Year's Day (one-day holiday), Spring Festival (three-day holiday), Labor Day (three-day holiday), and the National Day (three-day holiday); the second type is those when a part of all the citizens can enjoy the holiday, including Women's Day (half-day holiday only for women), Youth Day (half-day holiday only for the young people above 14 years old), Children's Day (one-day holiday for those below 13 years old), and Army's Day (half-day holiday for active armymen); the third type of statutory festivals and memorial days is those without any holiday, for example, July 1st Memorial Day for the establishment of the China Communist Party, July 7th Memorial Day for the beginning of the anti-Japanese War, September 3rd Memorial Day for the victory of anti-Japanese War, Tree-Planting Day, Teachers' Day, Nurses' Day, and Journalists' Day, and etc.

New Year's Day

Name: New Year's Day (*Yuan Dan* in Chinese pronunciation)
Date: January 1st

The concept of *"Nian"* (meaning "year" in Chinese) originally derived from agriculture production. In ancient times, people called the growth cycle of grain *"Nian"* (a year), which means, when grains get ripe one time, it is one year. In Xia Dynasty (2070-1600 BC) and Shang Dynasty (1600-1046 BC), Chinese people created Xia Calendar, by which people regarded the cycle of moon being full or not as a month, and divide one year into 12 months. The usage of the concept *"Nian"* started from Zhou Dynasty. Chinese people usually call the first day of a year *"Yuan Dan."* *"Yuan"* means "beginning," and *"Dan"* refers to the time of dawn, also refers to daytime. The combination of *"Yuan"* and *"Dan"* means the very beginning time, namely the first day of one year.

Originally, the first day of *Zheng Yue* (the first lunar month) was called *"Yuan Dan"* in China, but it was not unified what day should be the first day of *Zheng Yue*. And the dates of Chinese New Year's Day are not the same either in various dynasties. For instance, it was on the first day of *Zheng Yue* in Xia Dynasty, on the first day of the twelfth lunar month in Shang Dynasty, and on the first day of the eleventh lunar month in Zhou Dynasty. After Qin Shihuang (the first emperor in China, 259-210 BC) unified the six states, Qin Dynasty took the first day of the tenth lunar month as *"Yuan Dan,"* and this stipulation had been followed by the later dynasties since then. In 104 BC, Han Wudi (an emperor of Han Dynasty, 156-87 BC) accepted the advice of Sima Qian (c.145 or 135 BC-?) and some other people, and started to use *Taichu Calendar*, which is Chinese lunar calendar even used today. Like the calendar of Xia Dynasty, *Taichu Calendar* also took *Zheng Yue* as the beginning of one year, and adopted the 24 solar terms into it. Although all later dynasties made some change on it, they basically followed the calendar's blueprint and took the first day of *Zheng Yue* as *"Yuan Dan."*

After Xinhai Revolution in 1911, the government of Qing Dynasty was overthrown, the feudal rule of China was finally over, and Mr. Sun Zhongshan (or Sun Yat-sen, 1866-1925) established the government of the Republic of China (1912-1949) in Nanjing. The representatives of all provincial governors

Enormous "China net."

On New Year's Eve, people strike the bell and pray for a blessed New Year.

Annual New Year Concerts are becoming the fashion in numerous cities nowadays.

gathered together in Nanjing to discuss the problem of calendar. In order to be convenient for agriculture production and for statistics, the government stipulated that the lunar calendar will be used in common people's life, and the Gregorian calendar will be used in government, factories, schools, and social organizations. On September 27, 1949, the first session of Chinese People's Political Consultation Conference (CPPCC) passed a resolution, which formally stipulated January 1st of the Gregory calendar as "*Yuan Dan*" (namely the New Year's Day) and the first day of lunar calendar as "*Chun Jie*" (namely Spring Festival, also called the New Year's Day of lunar calendar).

Chinese people attach more importance to the New Year's Day of lunar calendar than to that of the Gregorian Calendar. Therefore, the celebrations for the New Year's Day are not so warm and big-scaled as those of *Chun Jie*. However, around the New Year's Day, people also have some big celebrations, such as orchestral concert and parties. Greeting cards are also presented to each other among friends, relatives and some organizations to express their good wishes.

March 8th Women's Day

Name: International Labor Women's Day
Date: March 8th

International Labor Women's Day, also called "the UN Day for Women's Right and International Peace" or "March 8th Day," is a glorious holiday to commemorate all the women's struggle throughout the world for peace, democracy, and liberation.

On March 8th, 1857, the women workers in the clothes and textile factories of New York held a demonstration to protest the non-humane working environment, 12-hour working system and low salary. The demonstrationists were sieged and finally dispelled by policemen. Two years later, and in March again, these women organized the first trade union.

On March 8th, 1908, 1,500 women gave a parade in New York City and asked for shortening the work time, improving the work wage, having the right for vote, and forbidding using child labor. The slogan they brought forward was "Bread and Rose," in which bread symbolized economic safeguard and rose symbolized better life quality.

On March 8th, 1909, the women workers in Chicago went on a great strike and held a protest demonstration. They demanded to increase wages, implement 8-hour work system, and get the right to vote.

In March 1910, the Second International Conference of Socialist Women from 17 countries was held in Copenhagen, Denmark. They discussed some important issues concerning opposing militaristic armament, protecting children's rights, struggling for 8-hour work system and women's rights for vote, and etc. Mrs. Clara Zetkin, a German socialist revolutionist and an international women movement leader, advocated that March 8th should be stipulated as International Women's Struggling Day so as to unite all the working women throughout the world together to oppose the imperialistic aggressive wars, oppose oppression, and struggle for women's own rights and liberation. This proposal was completely agreed at this conference, that March 8th would be set as International Labor Women's Day.

Receiving a holiday surprise from her husband, the wife flows off happy tears. The text on the board reads: "Happy Women's Day! I love you! Thank you for your dedication!"

In China, it was in 1924 that celebrations were held for the first time to commemorate the March 8th International Labor Women's Day. Presided by the famous women activist He Xiangning (1878-1972), Chinese women from all circles gathered together in Guangzhou to commemorate this Women's Day. They raised such slogans as "Down with imperialistic warlords," "Abolish multi-wife system," "Forbid concubinage," which showed their will of opposing imperialism, opposing feudal

In the splendid attire, Women of various nationalities gather and celebrate the March 8th Festival in front of the gate of the People's Great Hall.

system, and sticking up for women's rights. From then on, celebrations were held every year on this day. After the foundation of the People's Republic of China, the central government made a regulation that March 8th of every year would be a festival of Chinese women. On that day all the women enjoy a half-day holiday, and celebrations and activities will be held too.

1n 1977, the 32nd UN Congress formally determined March 8th as "the UN Day for Women's Rights and International Peace."

Tree-Planting Day

Name: Chinese Tree-Planting Day
Date: March 12th

Portrait of Sun Yat-sen.

Tree-Planting Day is a statutory festival which some countries set in order to inspire people's passions for planting and protecting trees, to increase the area of land covered by forests, and to protect the natural environment on which people depend for their living.

State Nebraska of the U.S. is the place where Tree-Planting Day was set at the earliest time. On April 10th, 1872, Sterling Morton, a famous American agriculturist, put forward the proposal of setting Tree-Planting Day at a meeting of the Garden Society of Nebraska. The state adopted his proposal. From the year of 1885, April 22nd was set as Tree-Planting Day of the state. From then on, the other states of the U.S. and all other countries had some response to this regulation.

After Xinhai Revolution of 1911, Mr. Sun Yat-sen, the Chinese leader of that time, put forward a plan of planting trees on a large scale in the northern and middle parts of China, and also gave a future picture of agriculture modernization. In 1924, he emphasized in a speech given in Guangzhou, "our research findings indicate that the basic way of avoid flood and drought is to plant trees and form forests. We need to have large areas of forests." Later in many works and speeches of his, he repeatedly stressed the hazard of damaging forests and the importance of

Little "gardeners" are planting azaleas on the Tree-Planting Day.

planting trees.

In 1915, in response to Sun Yat-sen's proposal, Beiyang government (Northern government) formally publicize a regulation that Pure Brightness Festival (April 5th) was adopted as Tree-Planting Day. From them on, China had its own Tree-Planting Festival. However, some time later, as Pure Brightness Festival is a time which is too late for tree-planting in the southern part of China, and also in order to commemorate Mr. Sun Yat-sen, the national government decided to take March 12th, the date when Mr, Sun Yat-sen passed away, as Tree-Planting Day.

In February 1979, the 6th session of the standing committee of the 5th NPC made a resolution that March 12th would be taken as Chinese Tree-Planting Day, and demanded the whole country to carry out tree-planting activities on this day, and the whole society to support the construction of forestry. In 1981, based on Deng Xiaoping (1904-1997)'s proposal, the 5th NPC passed the *Resolution on Launching a Campaign of Voluntary Tree-Planting throughout the Country*.

When March 12th Tree-Planting Day is approaching, people usually go outdoors to fulfill a citizens' obligation of planting trees. Deng Xiaoping, who was the active initiator of Chinese tree-planting movement, had planted trees in Tree-Planting Day continuously for eight years. People's sense of environment protection, harmonious development, social responsibility and rule of law is getting stronger and stronger in the campaign of voluntary tree-planting advocated by the government. Since December of 1981, the total number of trees planted voluntarily by the whole country has reached as many as 35 billion.

According to the statistics of the UN, there have been 50 countries so far which have set a Tree-Planting Day. Because of the difference of specific situation and geographical position of each country, the name and date of Tree-Planting Day in each country is also different from each other.

May 1st International Labor Day

Name: International Labor Day
Date: May 1st

May 1st International Labor Day is the common festival of all the proletariates and working people of the world. It originated from a great strike in Chicago of the U.S.

On May 1st, 1886, 216,000 workers in Chicago went on a great strike for the 8-hour working system. They finally won a victory after a hard bloody fight. To commemorate this great workers' strike, the Conference for Socialist Representatives was held in Paris, France, on July 14ᵗʰ, 1889. At the meeting French representatives proposed that May 1ˢᵗ of 1886, on which American workers strived for 8-hour working system, should be set as a common festival for international proletariats. This proposal was totally agreed by all the representatives and a historically significant resolution concerning it was passed. It was on that day that May 1ˢᵗ International Labor Day was born. The resolution of the conference was actively responded very soon by the workers all over the world. From then on, the working people of all countries usually had some congregations and paraded on the same day of every year to celebrate the festival.

It dates back to the year of 1918 that Chinese people started to celebrate the Labor Day. In this year, some progressive intellectuals distributed some handbills to introduce May 1ˢᵗ Labor Day in Shanghai, Suzhou, Hangzhou, Hankou and some other places. On May 1ˢᵗ, 1920, some workers in Beijing, Shanghai, Guangzhou, Jiujiang, Tangshan and other industrial cities gave a large-scale congregation and parade, which was the first celebration for May 1ˢᵗ Labor Day in Chinese history.

After the foundation of the PRC, the central government, namely the State Council, set May 1ˢᵗ as a statutory festival in December 1949, and regulated that the whole country takes a holiday on that day. People usually wore beautiful clothes for the festival, happily gathered at parks, theatres, and squares to take part in various celebrations and entertainment activities. And those

(Left) *Representatives of workers singing "We Workers Are Powerful."* (Right) *Telephone cards distributed by CNC for the Labor Day.*

Chinese Festivals

working people who had made outstanding contributions would be awarded on that day. On September 18th, 1999, the State Council made a new regulation to change the one-day holiday into a three-day holiday for the May 1st festival. From 2000, the total holiday extended into 7 days (the statutory 3-day holiday plus the two weekends before and after the May 1st Labor Day).

May 4th Youth Day

Name: Chinese Youth Day
Date: May 4th

Chinese Youth Day comes of May 4th Movement, the well-known anti-imperialistic and patriotic movement which took place in China in 1919.

After World War I, U.K., France, U.S., Japan, Italy and some other countries held a "Peace Conference" in Paris in 1919. Chinese government of that time also sent some representatives for the conference, and demanded that the imperial countries should abandon their privilege in China, Japan should cancel the "21 Items," an unequal treaty imposed by Japan, and China take back its sovereignty over Shandong which was occupied by Germany before the War and by Japan during the War. In May 1919, "Paris Conference" unfairly refused the reasonable request that China asked to abolish the unequal treat, and even decided to transfer the Germany's illegal privileges in Shandong Province to Japan. When the news passed back to China, the whole country got angry. On May 4th, about 3,000 students from various universities in Beijing congregated at Tian'anmen Square and held a student protest parade for the first time in the history. The students shouted out some patriotic slogans and presented a petition to the state president, but suppressed by the warlord government of that time. This suppression made angrier the people all over the country. A great number of students, workers and businessmen went on strike, and the students' demonstration and parade finally developed into a national-scale anti-imperialistic and patriotic movement. On June 10th, the warlord government

A historical picture of the May 4th Movement.

64

Students take an oath and release the red balloon in the adult ceremony.

had to compromise, and deposed Cao Rulin, Zhang Zongxiang, and Lu Zongyu who were regarded as committing a crime of quislingism. On June 28th, Chinese representatives at Paris Conference refused to sign the "Peace Treaty." This news passed throughout the world soon and the imperialistic countries were greatly shocked. So far, the direct goals brought forward in the movement were basically achieved.

May 4th Movement is a landmark event in Chinese history. It is not only a patriotic student movement, but also a new cultural movement with the characteristic of democracy and science against feudal culture. It was due to the influence of May 4th Movement that science, democracy and the usage of modern Chinese language were greatly advocated later.

May 4th Movement has reflected the strong will of Chinese people for safeguarding national independence and striving for democracy and freedom. In order to inherit and develop the spirit of patriotism, democracy and science of the May 4th Movement, the central government (the State Council) formally claimed in 1949 that May 4th would be Chinese Youth Day. In this festival, a variety of celebrations are held all over the country, such as gatherings, volunteer activities, social practices and some ceremonies for being an adult.

On Youth Day, all the youths above 14 years old in the country have a half-day holiday.

June 1ˢᵗ International Children's Day

Name: International Children's Day

Date: June 1ˢᵗ

June 1ˢᵗ Children's Day is a festival for the children all over the world. In August 1925, representatives from 54 countries gathered together in Geneva, Switzerland, to hold the International Conference for Children's Happiness, and passed a document, *Geneva Manifesto for Safeguarding Children*. This document involved various aspects about children issues, including the spiritual entertainment of children, the relief of poor children, the avoidance of dangerous work for children, children's acquisition of making a living, how to raise and educate children, and etc. Since this conference, governments of many countries had successively set "Children's Day," to inspire children and make them happy, and also to arouse the whole society's attention and protection for children.

The origin of the international festival was during the World War II. In June 1942, German Fascists shot about 140 male villagers above 16 years old and all the babies in a village of Czechoslovakia, and took all the women and 90 children to a concentration camp.

In order to mourn for all the children who died in this village and all over the world during the anti-Fascist War, in order to oppose the imperialistic warmonger slaughtering children, and in order to safeguard children's rights for survival, health care and education, the International Democratic Society of Women held a conference of its executive committee in Moscow in November 1949, formally made a resolution that June 1ˢᵗ of every year would be a festival for children all over the world, namely Children's Day.

Children draw a picture of one hundred meters long together on Children's Day.

Since 1931 in China, according to the advice of China's Charity Society, April 4ᵗʰ of every year had been the Children's Day. After the foundation of PRC, the central government regulated in 1949 that June 1ˢᵗ would be the Children's Day of New China.

At present, governments of all countries care for children's

Garden party full of children's laughter.

future and protect children's rights. In 1990, the UN passed the *Pact for Children's Rights*, and China is one of the countries that participated in drafting out the pact and signed on it. In the same year when the government ratified the *Pact for Children's Rights*, China enacted the *Law for Protecting Non-adults of the PRC*, which played an active role in safeguarding children's rights. Under the care of the government, the whole society has taken the responsibilities of protecting and educating children. They have good conditions for life, study and health care. They can grow up healthily and happily. Now on June 1st Children's Day, all the children under the age of 13 have a one-day holiday. In some places, the local government regulates that children's parents can also enjoy the one-day holiday. As "little super stars" of that day, children are usually accompanied by their parents to go to parks, zoos, pleasure grounds, or visit science & technology expositions, museums, and planetariums, or take part in some activities with special topics (such as the contest of Chinese calligraphy and drawings) in children's activity centers. In a word, the children fully enjoy themselves in this festival of their own.

August 1st Army's Day

Name: Army's Day (Memorial Day for the Foundation of PLA of China)
Date: August 1st

August 1st is the memorial day for the foundation of People's Liberation Army of the PRC.

At the beginning of the democratic revolution, led by Sun Yat-sen, Chinese Communist Party (CCP) and Chinese Kuomintang were allied. In April 1927, Chiang Kai-shek (1887-1975) of Kuomintang launched an anti-revolutionary coup d'etat, and wantonly slaughtered communists. Thus, the cooperation of Chinese Communist Party and Chinese Kuomintang broke up. In order to save revolution, about 20,000 people of northern expedition army, who were influenced by the CCP, led by Zhou Enlai (1898-1976), He Long (1896-1969), Ye Ting (1896-1946), Zhu De (1886-1976) and Liu Bocheng (1892-1986), started up an uprising in Nanchang, Jiangxi Province, on August 1st of that year, and gave the first shot to the rulers of Kuomintang, which marked the beginning of Chinese Communist Party leading the armed revolution independently. Shortly after the uprising army took over Nanchang city, it marched toward the southern Guangdong Province, and was finally dispersed by the enemy. A part of the army led by Zhu De and Chen Yi (1901-1972) arrived in Jinggangshan Mountain of Jiangxi Province in April 1928, joined forces with the army led by Mao Zedong (1893-

Honor Guards of Chinese People's Liberation Army.

Nanchang Uprising, a relief on the Monument of the People's Heroes that stands in Tian'anmen Square, Beijing. Photo by Dong Yu.

1976), and then formed the Chinese Red Army mainly consisting of workers and peasants. It was from then that the people's army led by Chinese Communist Party was established. Through the Long March, anti-Japanese War and Liberation War, this army gradually developed and got stronger, and finally became today's People's Liberation Army of China.

On June 26th, 1933, the central bureau of the Soviet area of the CCP made a resolution that August 1st would be set as a memorial day for the establishment of Chinese Red Army. On June 30th, 1933, the central military committee of the Red Army gave a relative command, pointing out that "On August 1st, 1927, Nanchang Insurrection, led by a proletariate party, the CCP, took place. This insurrection was the beginning of Land Revolution against imperialism, and the source of the valiant Red Army." On July 11th, the central authority organization of the revolutionary base area – the People's Committee of the central government held the 46th conference, and decided to ratify the advice of the central military committee of the Red Army that August 1st was adopted as the Memorial Day for the establishment of Chinese Red Army. From then on, when August 1st Army's Day was approaching, various activities to offer support to the army and show respect to their relatives were usually held.

Nanchang Uprising Monument, Nanchang, Jiangxi. Photo by Qian Jin.

After the foundation of Chinese People's Liberation Army, it still adopted August 1st as the Army's Day.

Teachers' Day

Name: Chinese Teachers' Day
Date: September 10th

Teachers' Day is one of the three occupational festivals in China. The other two occupational ones include Nurses' Day and Journalists' Day. From 1931, China had four Teachers' Day all together with various dates and qualities in various periods of time.

The earliest Teachers' Day appearing in Chinese history was in 1931. At that time, the well-known professors Tai Shuangqiu and Cheng Qibao, contacting some other people in the field of education, discussed and determined June 6th as Teachers' Day, and published the *Manifesto on Teachers' Day*, which presented three goals – bettering teachers' living conditions, safeguarding teachers' work, and improving teachers' qualities. This attempt to set a Teachers' Day was not admitted by the Kuomintang government of that time, but it did have some influence in the whole country.

Why the Kuomintang government did not admit the June 6th Teachers' Day was mainly due to the fact that June 6th Teachers' Day was set spontaneously by some teachers themselves. In 1939, the Kuomintang government decided to set August 27th, the birthday of ancient Chinese educator Confucius, as Teachers' Day, and issued for enforcement of Temporary Regulations on Setting Teachers' Day. However, this was not widely enacted throughout the country.

In 1951, the Ministry of Education and All-China Federation of Trade Unions made a resolution that May 1st International Labor Day was also set as Teachers' Day. Since teachers did not have individual celebration activities on this day, this Teachers' Day did not attract more attention either.

On December 9th of 1984, Professor Wang Zikun, an academician of Chinese Academy of Science and the president of a university, once again came up with the idea that "teachers should have their own festival," and told such an idea to *Beijing Evening Paper*. On the next day, *Beijing Evening Paper* published

Portrait of Confucius.

Kindergarten children are painting a "colored dress" for their teacher.

an article, reporting that President Wang Zikun advocated a series of activities to respect teachers and pay more attention to education. This article aroused a strong response among the readers. On December 15th, professors Zhong Jingwen, Qi Gong, Wang Zikun, Tao Dayong, Zhu Zhixian, Huang Ji, Zhao Qinghuan and some other people from Beijing Normal University formally proposed that Teachers' Day should be set. In order to keep up and develop the good tradition of "respecting teachers and attaching importance to education," and in order to improve the status of teachers, the ninth session of the standing committee of the 6th NPC made a resolution on January 21st, 1985, that September 10th would be set as Teachers' Day.

It is after careful consideration that September 10th has been adopted as Teachers' Day. September 10th is a time when students of primary schools, middle schools, colleges and universities started their new terms, and various schools show themselves a new scene and atmosphere. As soon as the new term starts, students can feel the atmosphere of respecting teachers and attaching importance to education, which can promote the establishment of a harmonious relationship between teachers and students. September 10th of 1985 is the first Teachers' Day after

71

New China resumed setting such a festival. The President Li Xiannian (1909-1992) wrote a greetings letter to all the teachers of the country. In Beijing, 10,000 people congregated to hold a celebration conference. During the festival, altogether 11,871 teaching groups and individual teachers were awarded provincial-level prizes in 20 provinces. From then on, Chinese teachers had their own unique festival.

National Day

Name: National Day
Date: October 1st

At three o'clock on October 1st, 1949, 300,000 people held a ceremony in Tian'anmen Square to celebrate the founding of People's Central Government of PRC. Chairman Mao Zedong gravely declared the founding of People's Central Government and of PRC and personally hoisted the first five-star flag. He read out the *Announcement of People's Central Government of PRC*, "People's Central Government of PRC is the only legal government to stand for all people of PRC. Our government is willing to establish diplomatic relationship with any foreign government that agrees to abide by the principles of equality, mutual benefit, mutual respect for territorial integrity, and so on." Then parade and folk procession were performed. Zhu De – Commander in chief – inspected marine, land and air force and announced *Order of Chinese People's Liberation Army Headquarter*, ordering the army to promptly clear all remaining armed forces of Kuomintang and to liberate all land that hasn't been liberated yet. On the same day, Beijing Xinhua broadcasting station conducted in Tian'anmen Square a live broadcast of the founding ceremony of PRC. That was the 1st large-scale live broadcast in the broadcasting history of Chinese people, other broadcasting stations all over China broadcasting synchronously.

October 1st, 1949, is the commemoration day of the founding of New China. It should be stated that in the opinion of many, a founding ceremony was held in Tian'anmen Square on that day that accommodated hundreds of thousands of soldiers and civilians. But in fact this impression is not accurate, because the ceremonies in Tian'anmen Square on October 1st, 1949, were establishing ceremonies of People's Central Government of PRC but not founding ceremonies of the country. As a matter of fact, the founding of PRC was announced a week before October 1st, which was September 21st, 1949. On that day, Mao Zedong – director of preparation committee of Chinese People's Political Consultative Conference – had announced the founding of New China in the opening address in the first session of the conference.

On October 1ˢᵗ, 1949, Chairman Mao Zedong announced to the world augustly that New China was founded.

Then what about the National Day of October 1ˢᵗ? On the first meeting of national committee's first session of Chinese People's Political Consultative Conference, some representative said "the founding of PRC should have a day for celebration. So I hope this session will decide October 1ˢᵗ as national holiday." Mao Zedong replied, "We have to propose to the government for it to decide." December 3ʳᵈ, 1949, the fourth session of People's Central Government committee passed *Decision on National Holiday of PRC*, stipulating that October 1ˢᵗ would be national holiday every year and this day was also affirmed to be the day of announcing the founding of PRC. From 1950, October 1ˢᵗ every year has been a highly celebrated holiday for people of all nationalities in China.

National holiday of PRC started from October 1ˢᵗ, 1949, and celebrations every year were given much political meaning. Before 1970, as major part of celebration, state banquet, military parade, fireworks and parade were held every year. There were grand meetings in Tian'anmen Square as well as in all provinces, regions and counties. In each meeting leaders of all levels made speech and workers, farmers and representatives of liberation army made speeches, fully expressing the love of people of walks for PRC. After the meeting there was usually a parade. Excited people held colorful triangular flags and shouted slogans when parading along streets for celebration.

In addition, when New China was founded, PRC Political Consultative Committee decided to list military parade as a major program in national holiday ceremony. From the founding ceremony, 13 military parades were held in the past 54 national holidays.

In 1960, the government decided to have "minor celebration every five years and major celebration every ten years with military parades" on the principle of economic construction. On the 20th national holiday in 1969, although it was a major celebration, no military parade was held, considering the negative influence of deploying armies and the limitation of national finances. 1979 was the 30th holiday which was also a major celebration, but reform and opening up just started and all waited to be recovered and reconstructed, so no military parade was held either. However, the government held a 4,000-people state banquet and all major parks had brand park-tour activities. Up to 1984, China had not had military parades on

The dignified raising flag ceremony on Tian'anmen Square.

national holidays for 24 years in a row. Based on Deng Xiaoping's suggestion, who was then the national leader, Chinese government decided to resume military parade and held a large-scale military parade ceremony in Tian'anmen Square that year, the 35th anniversary of the founding of PRC.

At the end of August 2004, Chinese government made new arrangements as to how to celebrate national holiday. That was the third time that government asked to celebrate economically after the founding of New China. In that year, the major arrangements of national holiday in Beijing included reception banquet, large-scale theatrical evening in celebration of the 55th anniversary of PRC, park-tour activities, theme activities about education of patriotism and revolutionary traditions for youths, and so on.

Crowd on the Great Wall during the National Day "Golden traveling week."

Since 2000, national holiday lasts seven days. Beside, economy is getting better and better, so people have larger room for choice in ways of relaxation and entertainment. More and more people choose to go on tours. They even go outside China to Southeastern Asia, Europe, North America, Japan, and so on for holidays. National holiday, Spring Festival and May Day holiday combine to create a situation where the three major "golden weeks for tourism" of the year co-exist and co-develop. They also give a push to the new "holiday economy" of tourism, transportation, telecom industry, gift industry, catering trade, and other industries that develop with the three major holidays.

"We climbed on the Tian'anmen gate on the National Day!"

75

Festivals of the Minorities

China is a united multi-ethnic state. So far, there are 56 ethnic groups identified and confirmed by the Central Government. Since the Han represent 92% of the whole population, China's other 55 ethnic groups are customarily referred to as the national minorities.

These ethnic minorities, namely, are Mongolian, Hui, Tibetan, Uygur, Miao, Yi, Zhuang, Bouyei, Korean, Manchu, Dong, Yao, Bai, Tujia, Hani, Kazak, Dai, Li, Lisu, Va, She, Gaoshan, Lahu, Shui, Dongxiang, Naxi, Jingpo, Kirgiz, Tu, Daur, Mulam, Qiang, Blang, Salar, Maonan, Gelao, Xibe, Achang, Pumi, Tajik, Nu, Ozbek, Russian, Ewenki, De'ang, Bonan, Yugur, Jing, Tatar, Drung, Oroqen, Hezhen, Moinba, Lhoba and Jino.

Among them, the largest group Zhuang has more than 15 million people, followed by Manchu, Hui, Uygur, Miao, Yi, Tujia, Mongolian, Tibetan, Bouyei, Dong, Yao, Korean, Bai, Hani, Kazak, Li, Dai and so on, each having a population more than one million. However, there are only thousands of people in the ethnic groups like Ewenki and Oroqen.

China's ethnic groups live together over vast areas while some live in individual concentrated communities in small areas. In some cases minority peoples can be found living in concentrated communities in areas inhabited mainly by the Han people, while in other cases the situation is just the other way round.

The Han people are found in all parts of the country, but mainly in the middle and lower reaches of the Yellow River, Yangtze River, Pearl River and the Northeast Plain. Most of the minority ethnic groups live in the border regions in the Northeast, Southwest and Northwest. The others are also everywhere in China. In many parts of China, ethnic groups including the Han live together and become dependent on each other.

The Han people have their own spoken and written language, known as the Chinese language, which is commonly used throughout China and is the working language of the United Nations. The Hui and Manchu minority ethnic groups also use the Han (Chinese) language. However, a total of 53 minority ethnic groups use spoken languages of their own; 23 minority ethnic groups have their own written languages.

Each minority ethnic group in China has its own long-time history and unique culture. They have different life styles, customs and habits. Clothes they wear, food they eat, houses they build, even the wedding ceremonies or funerals they hold differ from one to another. The traditions of these minority ethnic groups are highly respected and they have rights to reserve or evolve their traditions and customs on their own.

Naturally, minority people in China boast various festivals and almost every nationality has her own major festivals. Typical examples are the Tibetan New Year, Water-Splashing Festival for Dai people, and Torch Festival for Yi people, the Singing Carnival for Zhuang people and *Nadam* Fair for Mongolian people. All these festivals are colorful and charming. All the minority people in China enjoy freedom to celebrate their own festivals at their own will.

Nadam Fair

Name: *Nadam* Fair of the Mongol
Date: between July and August

In Mongolian, *Nadam* means recreation or game. The traditional annual festival is a grand gathering of the Mongolian people during the golden period of autumn between July and August when the grass on the meadows is ripe and the livestock in their best physical condition. The main events of a *Nadam* Fair are horseracing, wrestling, archery as well as theatrical performances. To the Mongolian people, the *Nadam* Fair is ancient, sacred, grand and full of fun. Nowadays, it has become a large-scale comprehensive gathering including sacrificial rites,

The exciting horse racing in the Nadam *Fair.*

celebrations, athletic sports, entertainment and trade. Agricultural products, by-products, native products and animal products from different prefectures are exchanged at the fair.

Most Mongolian people live in Inner Mongolia, Gansu, Qinghai, Xinjiang, Jilin and Liaoning. According to the fifth national census in 2000, there are 5.8139 million Mongolians across China. They have their own spoken and written language, which belongs to the Mongolian group of the Altaic language family. The Mongolians use three dialects: Inner Mongolian,

Barag-Buryat and Uirad. The Mongolian script was created in the early 13th century on the basis of the script of Huihu or ancient Uygur, which was revised and developed a century later into the form used to this day.

In 1206, Temujin (1162-1227) of the Mongolian tribe had a clan conference held on the bank of the Onon River, at which he was elected the Great Khan of all Mongols with the title of Genghis Khan. Since then, for the first time ever, northern China saw a powerful and sustainable ethnic group – The Mongolians. Between 1219 and 1260, the Mongolian army launched three massive expeditions, expanding the Mongolian empire into Central Asia and Europe. Genghis Khan died in 1227. In 1272, following more than 70 years of battles, his son Kublai Khan (1215-1294) founded the Yuan Dynasty. In 1279, Kublai Khan subdued the Southern Song, bringing the whole of China under his centralized rule.

As early as the beginning of the 13th century, Mongolian tribe chiefs started holding big gathering called *Nadam*. Historical records said Genghis Khan held a grand *Nadam* Fair focusing on archery after conquering Khwarizmi. Afterwards, the *Nadam* Fair became a regular major traditional event including archery, horseracing and wrestling, which are commonly called the Big Three Arts among Mongolians. During the Qing Dynasty, the *Nadam* Fair was held once in six months or in two years. The winners were prized with horses, camel, cow, sheep, brick tea or silk.

In the past, large-scale sacrificial rites were held at the beginning of a *Nadam* Fair with tribe seniors or local officials reciting eulogies. Nowadays, sacrificial rites have been reduced to a quite symbolic opening ceremony, even in Xinggan area in eastern Inner Mongolia where the *Nadam* Fair remains a densely traditional style.

Generally speaking, the *Nadam* Fair is held annually in July or August when the pastures are at their greenest and livestock are in their best condition. The period is also the best season for cattle trading in the area. Mongolians also used to celebrate the harvest and pray for a happy and prosperous life during the festival.

Traditionally, a *Nadam* Fair is a contest of the three ancient nomadic arts of wrestling, archery and horse racing.

Wrestling: the most popular and the widest-spreading game among Mongolians. In ancient times, the wrestling winners were hailed as heroes on the pastures and were often chosen by the nobles as their daughters' bridegrooms. For the Mongolian people, the wrestling is not only a game of strength, but also a game of wisdom.

Usually, the wrestler at a *Nadam* Fair will wear in tight, fully silver button-decorated leather vest and knee-high boots, with a necklace of red, yellow and blue ribbons. They entered the competition site in a kind of eagle-style pace, while singing battle

Mongolian wrestling.

songs loudly with big self-confidence. This scene is quite unforgettable.

Archery: Ancient Mongolians used arrows and bows for hunting and fighting. It was his imposing cavalries who are highly skillful at archery that helped Genghis Khan establish his vast empire. Therefore, since centuries ago, archery is a favorite game among Mongolians who regard bow and arrows as the symbol of manhood, the weapon and also the mascot they must carry with themselves everywhere. To watch archery competition at the *Nadam* Fair is quite an exciting experience: The competitors, wearing narrow-sleeved tight robes, bend their bows when riding galloping horses and shot arrows sharply at the center of targets.

Horse racing: the most eyeball-attracting event in a *Nadam* Fair. Mongolians grow up on horsebacks and horses thus play the most important part in their life. Every Mongolian loves to prove his worth by showing good horsemanship, which they pursue tirelessly since they are very young.

Aobao Sacrificial Rites

Aobao, also called *Dui Zi*, is a man-made pile of stones, which is usually built on the highland or hills in Mongolian pastures. They are quite common and often used as landmarks or bordering monuments in the pastures.

After the long-time evolvement, *Aobao* Sacrificial Rites have become ceremonies praying for the blessing of mountain gods, road gods, for the prosperous of livestock and family, for a safe journey and peaceful life, etc. The participators should walk around the *aobao* from its left to its right for three times, while distributing milk, wine, cream, cakes and sweets all onto the *aobao*.

Since the establishment of the Inner Mongolia Autonomous Region, the *Nadam* Fair becomes a real grand gathering of Mongolian people themselves with modern features and new facets developed. At the fair, thousands of people from all over Inner Mongolia and other Mongolian habitats gather together on the vast green fair site decorated with colorful flags. They wear their holiday best, drink koumiss, sing folk songs, eat roasted sheep, and play horse head-shaped instrument and dance from dark till dawn. There is a genuine touch of Mongolians' unrestrained enthusiasm. To this day, the *Nadam* Fair has become a joyful occasion to celebrate the harvest, the national unity and the achievements the Mongolians have made. It is also a comprehensive cultural and athletic meeting with focuses on traditional games but also including performances, exhibitions, information exchanges, trade and other activities.

Tibetan New Year

Name: Tibetan New Year
Date: the first day of the Tibetan calendar

Most Tibetans live in the Tibet Autonomous Region. There are also Tibetan communities in Qinghai, Gansu, Sichuan and Yunnan provinces.

The Tibetans originated from an agricultural tribe settling along the middle reaches of the Yarlung Zangbo River in Tibet. At the 7th century, King Songzan Gambo began to rule the whole of Tibet and made "Losha" (today's Lhasa) the capital of his slavery kingdom, which was called "Tubo" in Chinese historical documents dated in Tang and Song dynasties.

The Yuan Dynasty founded by the Mongols in the 13th century officially brought Tibet under the unified rule of the central government by instituting the administrative system, deploying armies, appointing civil and military officials, and fully exerting sovereign power there. This marked the beginning of the Chinese central authorities' overall control of Tibet.

The Tibetans, with a population of 5.146 million according

Sunning the Buddha on New Year's Day.

Chinese Festivals

to the fifth national census in 2000, have their own spoken and written language, which belongs to the Tibetan branch of the Tibeto-Burman group of the Sino-Tibetan language family. The Tibetan language has three major local dialects according to geographical divisions. The Tibetan script, an alphabetic system of writing, was created in the early 7th century and is used in all areas inhabited by Tibetans to this day.

The Tibetans believe in Lamaism, which belongs to the Mahayana School of Buddhism but assimilates some of the beliefs and rites of the local religion called "Bon." Lamaseries are all over Tibet and many Tibetan festivals bear a strong mark of religion. The Tibetans' social life and customs and habits bore obvious marks of their historical traditions and distinctive culture up to date.

The Tibetans have their own calendar, which was systematized in 1027. Written records show that the Tibetans invented their own calendar before 100 BC, which is called *Bon Calendar*. As the cultural exchanges between the Tibetans and the Han people enlarge, the Tibetan calendar finally becomes quite similar to the lunar calendar followed in areas home to members of the Han nationality. Under the rule of the Sagya Monastery, the Tibetan calendar was fixed as well as the ceremonies to celebrate the Tibetan New Year. It has remained unchanged since then.

The Tibetan calendar designates the years by uses of the five elements (metal, wood, water, fire and earth) and the 12 animals, which represent the 12 Earthly Branches. A year is thus divided into four seasons and 12 months, which have 29 or 30 days. For example, the year 2005 is called the Year of Wood Rooster and the year 2006 called the Year of Fire Dog according to the Tibetan calendar.

The Tibetan New Year is the most important festival in Tibet. Tibetans begin preparing for New Year's Day early in the twelfth month according to the Tibetan calendar. Besides food preparation, each household has to get ready a Five-Cereal Container which is a rich-carved colorful wooden box with fried highland barley mixed with butter inside and flowers made of butter and green shoots of highland barley above. This is done to pray for a bumper harvest and better life in the coming year.

Moreover, in preparation, Tibetans put highland barley seeds

Tibetan old women with prayer mills.

86

in a bowl of fresh water so that they can grow into one-or-two-inch-long green shoots when the New Year arrives. They also make fried wheat dough mixed with butter in various shapes as religious offerings and also for visiting guests.

On the eve of the Tibetan New Year, Tibetans clean up their houses, change door and window curtains, set up brand-new prayer flags on the roof and paint patterns symbolizing eternity and good luck on the gates with lime. In the evening, all family members reunite together and an "**auspicious dinner**" is offered. This dinner's main meal is dough drops known as Gutu in Tibetan, which include stone, wool, hot pepper, charcoal or coins inside. These items are said to be able to foretell the nature of and future fortunes of the person who eats them. For example, stone implies a cruel heart, wool stands for a soft heart, charcoal for a black heart, hot pepper for tough talking and coins for good fortune…

The Tibetan people usually don't go out or visit each other on the first day of the Tibetan New Year. From the second day, they will dress in their holiday best and extend greeting with the auspicious words "*tashi delek*" to each other. Mass singing and dancing, as well as traditional Tibetan operas, are performed in towns and villages across Tibet during the period. On the 15th day, religious activities are held in the large part of Tibetan areas.

Shoton Festival

Name: Tibetan *Shoton* Festival

Date: August (the first day of the seventh month of the Tibetan calendar)

Tibetan opera performance.

The Shoton Festival, also known as the Tibetan Opera Festival, is one of the grandest traditional festivals in Tibet. In the Tibetan language, "*Sho*" means yogurt and "*Ton*" means banquet. Therefore, the *Shoton* Festival is a festival of yogurt banquet. However, as time past, the *Shoton* Festival becomes a festival of traditional Tibetan operas. It is mainly celebrated in Lhasa and Xigaze.

The festival was a purely religious event prior to the 17th

century. The founder of the *Gelugpa* (Yellow Sect of Buddhism), Tsongkhapa regulates that lamas can cultivate themselves only in monasteries between the 15th and 30th of the sixth month in Tibetan calendar so as to avoid treading and killing tiny lives. The ban will be lifted on the first day of the seventh month according to Tibetan calendar then all lamas go outdoors, accept yogurt served by local people and then enjoy entertainment of folk songs and dances. This is said to be the origin of the *Shoton* Festival.

In early days, Drepung Monastery was the center of the *Shoton* Festival. That's why it was also called the Drepung *Shoton* Festival at the time. In the middle of 17th century, the Fifth Dalai Lama moved his residence from Drepung Monastery to the Potala Palace and added opera performance to this festival. At that time, **Tibetan operas** were first performed at Drepung Monastery on the 30th of the sixth month according to Tibetan calendar and moved into the Potala Palace to perform for Dalai Lama on the next day.

However, after Lhasa's Norbulingka was built in the early 18th century as the summer residence of the Dalai Lama, it soon

Tibetan opera performance.

became the main venue of the *Shoton* Festival. Ordinary people have since been permitted to visit Norbulingka during the festival days and the very same rituals remain in place even today.

During the festival, stage performances and other recreational activities last for days in Norbulingka, creating an extra-vibrant scene. Tibetan opera troupes or folk dance groups from Tibet, Qinghai, Gansu, Sichuan and Yunnan all come to perform. Tens of thousands of people, carrying colorful bundled wrapped in cloth and buckets of highland barley wine with them, rushed into tent-dotted Norbulingka. On carpets under green trees or beside multi-colored tents, with wine, food and desserts in front, they chat, drink, sing and dance all day.

In recent years, major cultural events, academic seminars and commodity exchanges are also held during the *Shoton* Festival, giving it a more comprehensive and influential role in Tibetans' social life.

Tibetan opera performance.

Bathing Festival

Name: Tibetan Bathing Festival
Date: from the sixth to the 12th of the seventh month of the Tibetan calendar

The Tibetan Bathing Festival is one of traditional festivals in Tibet. Since it lasts seven days, it is also known as the Bathing Week.

The seventh month of the Tibetan calendar is thought the best time for bathing in Tibet. It is the time when the rain season has just ended and the sunshine has become caressing. What's more, the water temperature near riverbanks will exceed 20 degrees centigrade at the time.

Therefore, when the sacred planet Venus appears for one week in the southern sky, all the people in Tibet go into the river for bathing. They take carts or ride horses, bring buttered tea, wine and food together with them, set up tents or big umbrellas along rivers and then enjoy the whole day of bathing.

Usually, Tibetans start the day with washing their quilts,

Tibetan boys bathing in the Yarlung-zangbo River.

clothes and shoes in the river first. At the noontime, when the temperature of the river water goes up, they jump into the river naked. Male and female, young and old, swim, play games and bath themselves all together. In the afternoon, most people like having a party inside tents or under trees, where they drink, sing, dance and make a lot of fun until Venue reappear in the sky. They then pack up everything they bring and go back home separately.

The Bathing Festival has at least seven or eight hundred years of history in Tibet where prevails many legends about its origin. Here is one of the stories: Once upon a time, there was a great doctor living in Tibet called the Medicine King due to his magic skill. When he died, he became a god living in the heaven. One year, a terrible epidemic struck the whole Tibetan area, killing numerous people and cattle. Tibetans then turned to the Medicine King, praying for his help to relieve their distress. When the Medicine King heard their praying, he turned himself into a bright star. When the star shone over the hills, all plants on the hills became medicine. When the star shone over the rivers, the water in the river was turned into medicine liquid, too.

In this night, everyone in Tibet had the same dream: a new bright star rose in the sky over southeastern Lhasa and a dark slim girl went into the clear Lhasa River to bathe herself in starlight. When she got out of the water, she became healthy and beautiful. It was widely believed that the dream was a magic implication given by the Medicine King himself and Tibetans then all went into the river to bathe themselves. After seven days, the new star disappeared from the sky, together with the epidemic on the earth. All the sick had recovered from their illness. Since then, Tibetans used to bathe themselves in the river during this seven-day period and later developed it into a festival.

Tibetan astronomical documents say that at the time between the end of summer and the beginning of autumn, the river water is sweet, cool, soft, light, clear and not smelly. Drinking it will do harm neither to throat nor to abdomen. Therefore, the Bathing Festival is said the best time for Tibetans to get bath and cleaning.

Fast-Breaking Festival

Name: Fast-Breaking Festival
Date: the first day of Shawwal, the tenth month of the Islamic calendar

The Festival of Fast-Breaking is one of the three major Islamic festivals and grandly celebrated by the Hui, Uygur, Kazak, Ozbek, Tajik, Tartar, Kirgiz, Salar, Dongxiang and Bonan people. Every September according to Islamic calendar is called Ramadan, which lasts for 29 or 30 days. During this period, Muslim people must finish their

Thousands of Hui Muslims go to the mosque for prayers in their festival best.

pre-fasting meal before sunrise and they are not allowed to eat or drink anything until the sun goes down. In addition, all Muslim people are supposed to curb all their personal desires, including that of sexual infercourse, and practice abstinence during this time in order to show their allegiance to Allah. Children, sick people, elderly people and women who are undergoing menstruate are allowed not to practice fasting but they should limit their diet and must not eat or drink in public. In the evening when the bells in the mosques ring, people could suspend their fasting and begin to have their meal.

The beginning and the end of the fasting month of Ramadan are strictly according to the appearance of the crescent. When the month of Ramadan ends, Muslims will celebrate the Fast-

Frying sanzi.

Breaking Festival.

According to the Koran, in the early days of Islamism, Muhammad, the Messenger of Allah, would mark the end of the fasting month of Ramadan by taking a bath, putting on clean clothes, walking to the outskirts of the city together with his Muslim followers, and handing out fast-breaking donations by way of atonement. This practice gradually evolved into one of the three major Islamic festivals celebrated by all the Muslims in the world.

On the morning of the festival, adult Muslims **take baths** and change into their festival best before **going to the mosque for prayers**. Then they begin visiting relatives and friends, extend greetings to each other, and hand out deep-fried dough twists, fried doughnuts, almonds, tea and fruit as a form of celebration. It is also a common practice for Muslims to whitewash their houses, clean up their yard, and have haircut and bath before the festival.

Corban Festival

Name: Corban Festival
Date: the tenth day of *Zhuld Hijja*, the twelfth month of the Islamic
calendar

The Corban Festival, an annual major traditional Islamic festival, falls on the tenth of the twelfth month of the Islamic calendar and is celebrated by Chinese minority nationalities that believe in Islam, including Hui, Uygur, Kazak, Ozbek, Tajik, Tartar, Kirgiz, Salar, Dongxiang and Bonan. It is called *Eid-al-Adjha* in Arabic. *Eid* means festival and *Adjha,* sacrifice. Therefore this day is also called Corban.

Butchering some oxen and sheep on Corban.

According to Islamic legend, once in a year, Muslims slaughtered a certain number of cattle and donated them to other people so as to show their sincere faith in Allah. Ibrahim, an prophet, once promised in public that he would slaughter his son as a sacrifice if Allah asked him to do so. In a dream, Ibrahim got Allah's divine message for him to practice his promise by slaughtering his son as a sacrifice. The dream repeated several times and finally, Ibrahim painfully made up his mind. On the next day, the tenth day of the final month according to the Islamic calendar, a tearful Ibrahim took his son to a hilltop. When he was about to carry out the order, a messenger sent by Allah descended with a sheep, and asked Ibrahim to sacrifice the sheep instead of his own son. Since then the Muslims have been marking the day by **slaughtering sheep**. This gradually evolved into the Corban festival, one of the most important Islamic festivals. .

During Corban, all Islamic families would clean up their houses and be busy making various cakes for the festival. All families that possess cattle exceeding a certain number would butcher some sheep, camels or oxen. It is regulated that the sheep to be slaughtered must be fostered more than one year and the oxen, more than two years. These families could keep one-third of the slaughtered cattle for themselves and distribute the rest to the poorest people and relatives.

In the morning of Corban, Islamic people would tidy their

Muslims knock the iron casing drum to celebrate the holiday.

clothes after taking a bath and **listen to imams' interpretation of Koran** in the mosques. It is the largest gathering in the mosques throughout a year. After prayers and rites, all the families will go to graveyard to pay tribute to their late beloved on the day.

Meanwhile, Corban also provides an optimum opportunity for conversation during which many Islamic people get together and share mutton, cakes, melons and fruits with others.

In Xinjiang Uygur Autonomous Region, Muslims are given three days as holidays to celebrate the Corban Festival. In Ningxia Hui Autonomous Region, all the governmental staff and employees, no matter they are Muslims or not, are given one day leave on Corban. Islamic associations across China also organize gatherings during the Corban Festival.

Torch Festival

Name: Torch Festival for Yi people
Date: the 24th of the sixth lunar month

With a population of 7.7623 million according to the 2000 national census, the Yi ethnic group lives mainly in Yunnan, Sichuan, Guizhou and Guangxi. The Yi language belongs to the Yi branch of the Tibeto-Burman group of the Sino-Tibetan language family and has six dialects. Yi characters, as the earliest syllabic script in China, were formed in the 13th century and more than 1,000 of them are still commonly used today.

The Yi people used to believe in many gods and worshiped ancestors. In Yunnan and Guizhou, many Yi people accept the influence of Buddhism and Taoism.

The Yi people have many traditional festivals, of which the Torch Festival is the grandest and the most important. It is also known as "the *Xinghui* (return of the stars) Festival." The festival has several origins according to different legends. A popular legend is about a wrestling contest between an ancient Yi hero and a god on the 24th of the sixth lunar month. Both of them had great strength but finally, the Yi hero wrestled and killed the god, leaving another god very angry. In revenge, the god sent locusts in immense swarms onto the earth and ate up almost all the corps in three days and three nights. The Yi people had to hold aloft torches together to drive locusts away. All the locusts were burnt to death during the three days and three nights of torch burning. From this time on, Yi people light torches on that day with intentions to kill harmful insects and ensure a bumper harvest.

Usually, Yi people start preparation for the arrival of the Torch Festival one month in advance. Children wander around hills and wild fields picking up dry, long and straight wormwoods for torch making. In the Liang Mountain area, Yi people usually only use wormwood, instead of bamboo shoots or pine branches, to make torches since they believe wormwood can help eliminate the evils. The number of torches prepared depends on how many members there are in the family. Usually, they will prepare three torches for one person, and of course, everyone wishes to have more and longer torches prepared for them.

Yi younsters singing and dancing.

At the time, parents need to prepare the food for sacrificial rites and holiday clothes for every family member. Girls need to get colorful turban and skirts in ready... Some girls are even busy at making Yi-style suits, waistbands or embroidered wallets for their lovers. Young men also buy silver earrings, blue capes or yellow umbrellas for girls they have fallen in love with. Every household purchases a large quantity of festival food including wine, sweets, noodle and fruit, while the whole village as a whole will purchase one cow or several cows and kill them during the festival as sacrifices for the Fire God.

Finally, the day of the 24th of the sixth lunar month arrives. The Yi people first clean their houses in the morning on that day. Then, everyone dresses in holiday best. Women are busy at cooking; men are busy at cow killing and beef distribution. The Yi people believe that eating beef on that day will bring them good luck and peaceful life throughout the whole coming year.

When night falls, the Yi people will have a grand family dinner and worship their ancestors and gods. Then the **torch parade** begins. Men and women of all ages hold aloft torches, shout auspicious words and walk around their houses and fields. Torches wind like so many flying fire dragons in the hills, illuminating fields and villages, dispelling evil.

What's more, all the villagers, in their holiday best, will gather at the main festival site, putting their torches together to make a big bonfire. Their **bonfire party** usually lasts till the next morning, young Yi men blowing flutes, plucking moon-shaped instruments and three-stringed guitars while dancing, young women dancing to the rhythm, clapping their hands. Cheerful flames leap up to the sky, crackling and spluttering. Shouts of joy together with the sound of the gongs and drums make a sea of rejoicing.

In the daytime, the Yi people watch wrestling, horse race, bullfight and other performances, giving the traditional festival more content. The festival now combines the traditional ceremony, tourism with trade negotiation and investment attraction and has become more colorful.

Many other ethnic groups including Bai, Naxi, Hani, Lahu and Pumi also celebrate the Torch Festival.

The night of the Torch Festival.

Pan Wang Festival

Name: *Pan Wang* (King Pan) Festival for the Yao people
Date: the 16th of the tenth lunar month

The Yao ethnic group, with a population of 2.6374 million according to the national census in 2000, is mainly scattered in the mountain areas in the Guangxi Zhuang Autonomous Region, as well as Hunan, Yunnan, Guangdong and Guizhou provinces. The Yao people have their own spoken language and many Yaos are also familiar with the Han and Zhuang languages. Yao does not appear in a written form, so there is a common use of written Chinese.

King Pan (*Pan Wang*) is regarded as the ancestor of the Yao ethnic group. For this reason, the Yao people celebrate this grand traditional festival to pay tribute to their ancestors. They also hold large-scale singing fair during the festival.

According to a legend, in the far ancient time, there was a war between King Ping of the Yao Mountain and King Gao. In order to win the war, King Ping offered his most beautiful daughter, the third princess, in marriage to whoever could bring back King Gao's head.

The Yao troops on parade with a huge portrait of the King Pan.

Unexpectedly, on the following day, a dragon-dog took the head of King Gao in its mouth to see King Ping. King Ping kept his promise so that the dragon-dog married the princess. However, the dragon-dog, whose name is Pan Hu, wanted to become a human being. He then asked the princess to steam him for seven days and seven nights. After six days and six nights of steaming, in fear that her husband was steamed to death, the princess opened the steam box, finding her husband turning into a strongly built man. After that, Pan Hu was sent by his father-in-law to rule the Kuaji Mountain as King Pan. Years passes, the couple raised six sons and six daughters, who later became the ancestors of 12 clans of Yao.

One day, while hunting in the mountains, Pan was run down from a cliff by an antelope and died in the accident. To remember their father, the children caught the antelope and made a drum out of the antelope's hide, which they beat sharply to express their anger and sorrow in their loss. This legend is believed to be the origin of the *Pan Wang* Festival. Since Pan was originally a dragon-dog, up to this day, eating dog is a very taboo for the Yao people.

Nowadays, *Pan Wang* Festival has gradually evolved into a holiday of great joy for the Yao group to celebrate a good harvest and worship their ancestors. Young Yao people **sing love songs** to select a sweetheart or to express their love for each other.

Danu Festival

Name: *Danu* Festival for Yao people
Date: the 29ᵗʰ of the fifth lunar month

The *Danu* Festival, also known as the Ancestral Mother Festival or the Yao New Year, is one of the grandest traditional festivals of the Yao ethnic group. It is scheduled for the 29ᵗʰ of the fifth lunar month. However, the Yao people don't celebrate this festival annually. They only hold the festival once in two or three, or even five years. In some Yao communities, the *Danu* Festival is celebrated once in every 12 or 13 years.

There is a widely spreading legend about the origin of this festival. In the far ancient time, there were two great magic mountains facing each other. The left one, looking like a great warrior, was called Buluosi. In contrast, the right one looked like a young girl in dress and was thus called Miluotuo. Every year they became a little bit closer. So after 995 years, the two mountains were actually approaching each other. On the 29ᵗʰ of the fifth lunar month of this year, a deafening thunderbolt suddenly struck the earth. Exactly at the same time, the two mountains were cracked. A man called Buluosi came out from the mountain Buluosi, while a woman called Miluotuo out from the mountain sharing same name. They married and gave birth to three daughters. When Miluotuo was aged, she told her three daughters: "Children, now that you have grown up, you have to live on your own." Therefore, her eldest daughter, carrying ploughs and harrows, settled down in plains and live on cultivation. Her offspring are the Han people. The second-eldest daughter left with a burden of books and her

The Yao men beating copper drums.

children fostered the Zhuang ethnic group. The youngest daughter, taking millet and hoes, developed paddy fields and planted different kinds of crops inside mountains. She became the ancestor of the Yao nationalities. Soon afterwards, the youngest daughter came back to her mother's home in tears, telling Miluotuo that the crops she grew were eaten up by field mice, beasts and birds. To try to help her youngest daughter, Miluotuo gave her a copper drum and a cat. In the following year, beasts and birds came back onto the third daughter's fields. But this time, following her mother's advice, the youngest daughter beat the copper drum and scared birds and beasts away. Meanwhile, the cat caught all the field mice. A good harvest was thus guaranteed in that year.

Since then, on every 29th of the fifth lunar month, the birthday of Miluotuo, the three daughters carried lavish gifts and came back home to join their mother and celebrate harvest. This finally evolves into a festival celebrated by the Yao people. *Danu* means "do not forget."

Before the *Danu* festival, all the Yao families will clean up their houses, prepare sticky rice cakes and rice wine and slaughter pigs and lambs to entertain their relatives and friends with lavish food and dishes. On the festival day, they will gather at the village common ground, singing, dancing, beating copper drums, blowing *suona* horn (a woodwind instrument), performing martial arts and playing ball games.

Among all the festive activities, **copper drum dance**, usually involving two men and a woman, is always the top attraction. The bold and unreserved dancing combines superbly with the rhythmic, sonorous tunes of the copper drums. The best drum player will be given the title of the King of Drum-beating and be congratulated by all the people on the scene.

After the copper drum dance, the Yao people set off dozens of or even hundreds of powerful **firecrackers** all at the same time in the village ground. The person who ignites the biggest number of firecrackers will be hailed as a hero.

Some Zhuang ethnic communities in the Guangxi Zhuang Autonomous Region also celebrate the *Danu* Festival.

Miao Dragon Boat Festival

Name: Dragon Boat Festival for the Miao people
Date: between the 24th and 27th of the fifth lunar month

The Mao ethnic group has a population of 8.9401 million according to the fifth national census carried in 2000. They are mainly scattered in Guizhou, Hunan, Yunnan, Sichuan, Guangxi, Hubei and Hainan.

101

Dragon Boats of the Miao Ethnic Group.

The Miao people have their own language that belongs to the Miao-Yao group of the Sino-Tibetan language family. They used to believe in many gods and worship their ancestors and nature's power. In their belief, gods or evil ghosts possess irresistible power and they need gods and their ancestors' blessings so as to get fortune and children, expel evil spirits and get rid of diseases.

The Han people celebrate the Dragon Boat Festival on the fifth day of the fifth lunar month every year to honor the memory of the patriotic poet Qu Yuan. However, the Miao Dragon Boat Festival, held later in the same month, has its own origin.

It is said, once upon a time, there lived a big black dragon in the Doushui River. The dragon was very cruel to people living along the river. At the time, an old fisherman lived with his only son along the river. One day in the fifth lunar month, the dragon kidnapped the son who was fishing on the river at the time. Hearing the news, the old fisherman, in great anger and sorrow, made up his mind to kill the dragon and save his son. Carrying a steel knife and kindling, the old man dived into the dragon cave deep under the sea. Having fought with the dragon for nine days and nine nights, the old man finally chopped the dragon into three pieces, saved his son out of the dragon cave and set fire the dragon cave.

Suddenly, thick smokes hung over the Doushui River where the corpse of the dragon drifted downwards. The heaven and the earth were in a state of chaos and darkness. Fortunately, at the time, a Miao girl came out to the riverbank to fetch water. She happened to drop her wooden ladle into the river. The girl immediately used her shoulder pole to get the ladle back. When the shoulder pole reached the

The Miao men wearing splendid attire are rowing the boat as fast as possible.

ladle in the water, with a splash, the heaven became bright again all of a sudden. The darkness disappeared and the earth embraced the sunshine again.

To commemorate the heroic deeds by the old fisherman and the girl, the Miao people hold celebrations from the 24th to 27th of the fifth lunar month by organizing **dragon-shaped boat rowing contests** along the Doushui River.

A dragon boat made by the Miao people, unlike the one used by the Han people which is just one larger and longer boat, is in reality a body made up with three canoes bound together – one large in the middle and two small on the sides. All of them are made of fir trees. The middle one is called mother boat or the main boat, while the other two known as son boats or boats attached. The bow of the middle one is decorated with a more-than-one-meter-high carved dragonhead, which is made from the trunk of a weep willow tree and painted colorfully. These dragon boats are actually exquisite and interesting craftwork.

On the day of the contest, every dragon boat is painted brand new and decorated with colorful flags. In each boat, the coxswain rides straddling the dragon's neck on the bow of the mother boat, beats the drum to set the pace for the oarsmen behind him. The oarsmen all wear horsetail-shaped hats, blue jackets and trousers, and embroidered waistbands pinned with silver ornaments. They look very powerful.

The contest starts. The coxswain beats drum with exciting rhythms, and the oarsmen row the boat as fast as possible while singing folk songs altogether. For audience on the riverbanks, it seems as if dozens of real dragons were riding the waves and forwarding quickly in the river.

Up to this day, some unique customs are still kept when the Miao people celebrate the Dragon Boat Festival. For example, villagers are allowed to send their boats down the river after the 16th before the festival, provided that they have finished weeding their fields. The earlier appearance of the boats on the river testifies to their efficiency. The diligent farmers consider it a shame not to finish weeding before the festival begins.

What's more, no matter how bad some oarsmen get on in daily life, they will shake hands once they are on board and cooperate with each other as one man during the contest. At the end of the contest route, the organizers will put a big duck into the river, which is then chased after by all the oarsmen arriving the final stop. The scene is just joyful.

Every Miao family attaches great importance to the Dragon Boat Festival and takes great care of their dragon boats. A special wooden-framed shelter with tile roof to house dragon boats has been built in every Miao village. Because of the well keeping, a Miao dragon boat can survive dozens of years, even more than one hundred years.

Flowery Mountains Festival

Name: Flowery Mountains Festival for the Miao people
Date: between the second and seventh day of the first lunar month

The Miao people living in Yunnan and some other places celebrate the festival, also known as the Festival of Treading the Flowery Mountains. During this annual festival, thousands of Miao people will go to the open hillsides among their villages and hold various festive activities.

Lusheng *dancing of the Miao ethnic group.*

The so-called "Flowery Pole" is always the mark of the festival. Usually, it is made from long, straight pine or cypress trees. Colorful flags and prizes for pole climbing like sweets and *lusheng* (a kind of reed pipe wind instrument) are hung about one meter lower from the top of the pole. The person who volunteers to set up the flowery pole before the first dawn of the festival will be widely recognized as a kind-hearted person. It is this person who takes responsibility to toast festival attendees and officially declare the beginning of the festival followed by the drum and gong beating and firecracker explosions.

At the time, the festive site, full of flowers and colorful flags, is just a sea of singing and dancing. Activities such as folk song singing, *lusheng* dancing, lion dancing and bull fighting are held one after another.

The festival offers a wonderful chance for young Miao people to find their sweethearts. Once falling in love, the young man will present his lover flowery embroidered puttees and waistbands as gifts, while the girls give out scarf and turbans they embroider themselves.

The Miao people in northeastern and southern Yunnan celebrate this festival on the sixth day of the sixth lunar month. Legend has it that, in ancient times, the Miao people were distressed about their ancestors' suffering. Once on this date, their ancestors made an appearance and told them not to be too distressed. Instead, the ancestors said they should cheer up, dance and **play *lusheng***. After that, suddenly a flower dropped to a tree on a hilltop from heaven. Then everyone danced around the tree, playing *lusheng* and singing songs. That year they had a bumper harvest.

Since then, they celebrate the festival on the date every year. Their celebration includes singing, *lusheng* dancing, bull fighting, lion dancing and the **climbing of the flowery pole** contest, in which the champion is awarded a pig head and fine wine. The winner of lion dancing will also be awarded a pig head and wine.

Water-Splashing Festival

Name: Water-Splashing Festival for the Dai people
Date: between the sixth day of the sixth Dai month and the seventh day of the seventh
      Dai month (around mid-April)

The majority of the Dai people live in the Xishuangbanna (Sipsongpanna) Dai Autonomous Prefecture in southernmost Yunnan Province. According to the fifth national census in 2000, the Dai population totaled 1.16 million.

The religion of the Dai is Hinayana (Theravada) Buddhism. The Dai also take part in animistic worship by offering sacrifices to spirits and ancestors.

At age seven or eight, many Dai boys become a *"keyong"* (a novice) and are sent to the village monastery to learn the Buddhist and doctrines before they join the community as a *"panan"* (child monk). Most Dai return to the secular life around age 17 or 18 and then marry.

There are at least five dialects of Dai in Yunnan. The more popular scripts later formed the basis of the current Xishuangbanna and Dehong Dai writing. After 1949 the Chinese developed a new simplified Dai script for use among the Dais.

Splashing blessings.

The Dai young girls celebrate the Water-splashing Festival joyfully.

The Water-splashing Festival, the New Year by the Dai calendar, held in the last ten days of the sixth month or early in the seventh month of the Dai calendar (April), usually lasts three to five days.

About the origin of the festival, legend has it that once upon a time, there was a "demon of fire" who brought all the pains and sufferings to the local people. He even forced seven women, one after another, to marry him. However, the seven women he married turned out to have the guts to kill him. One day, the most daring and the youngest woman of the seven strapped the devil's neck with his own long hair. The head of the devil fell to the ground and started rolling around. And whatever the burning head rolled over were set ablaze.

Former Premier Zhou Enlai celebrated the Water-splashing Festival together with the Dai people in Xishuangbanna (Sipsongpanna).

In order to put down the fire, the seven women hold the devil's blazing head in their arms, and they decided to hold the post in turn, each for one year. At the time of New Year when they switch shifts, local people would gather to splash water on the exhausted woman in a hope to wash the blood and dirt off her and refresh her. Today, the Dai people splash water at each other to commemorate the courageous act of these women who brought peace and happiness to them.

The first day of the festival is the New Year's Eve. On this day, the Dai people hold the "**ascending high**" competition and **dragon boat races**. The things that are "ascending high" are a self-made "rockets" – bamboos with gunpowder in them – which were "fired" into the sky and left a curve of smoke behind.

The second day is a day for break. It is a day belongs neither to the old year nor to the new year. It is simply a day for break and people usually stay home or go hunting in the mountains.

The third day is "the king of days." In the morning, people put on their best clothes and go to temples to pray for the good luck, big fortune and even more children in the New Year. In the afternoon, women will clean the statues of Buddha with water. Shortly after that, **water splashing** at people really begins.

Talking about water splashing, there is a "civilized way" and a "violent way." Being civilized, the Dai people dip flower branches in water and sprinkle the water on one another for blessing. But being violent, people use washbasins and buckets to splash water on others. And the more water one is splashed on, the happier and luckier one will be in the new year.

The festival culminate later in the day as the Dai people start singing, dancing and drinking late into the night.

Besides the traditional games such as "ascending high" and dragon boat races, new activities have been going on during the festival, such as cockfight, setting free balloons, going to amusement park and exchanging commodities, etc.

Third Month Street Fair

Name: Third Month Street Fair for the Bai people
Date: the 15th to 21st of the third lunar month

Bai is an ethnic group with a long history and unique culture inhabited in the Bai Autonomous Prefecture of Dali, Yunnan Province. The population totaled 1.86 million according to the fifth national census in 2005. The Bais have their own language, which belongs to Tibeto-Burman, a language group

A Bai woman is selling wax printing handicrafts on the Third Month Street.

The Third Month Street.

of the Sino-Tibetan language family. Most of them know Chinese.

The Street Fair is the grandest show of the year for the Bais. Held from the 15th day to the 21st day of the third lunar month every year at the foot of the Mount Diancang Shan, west to the ancient city of Dali, the Bais are holding the festival mainly pray for a good harvest.

The Third Month Street is also named the Market of *Guanyin*, literally the Goddess of Mercy. Legend has it that back in the period of Nanzhao State (938-1253), the Goddess of Mercy came to Dali to speak on Buddhism on the 15th of the third lunar month, and then the Third Month Street became a temple fair for loyal believers to pay homage. As time went, for Dali's strategic location, the city became a prosperous trade market in the region and a grand festival for the local people.

Another legend is about the existence of a "trade fair on the moon." It is said that the third princess of Dali fell in love with a young fisherman. On the 15th of the third lunar month, the two went to the moon to buy fishing net and other working instruments but returned home empty-handed. The local people somehow managed to relocate the trade fair to the earth and then the trade fair began in Dali. Until now, the Bais still call the Third Month Street the "Moon Street."

The traditional commodities traded at the fair are horses, mules, tea, medicine etc. But now, both the trading place and the commodities have changed a lot. In addition to the exchange of commodities, there are horse racing, performance of operas,

Still of the movie "Five Golden Flowers."

folk singing and dancing, attracting tens of thousands of visitors, including those from other Chinese ethnic groups as well as tourists from over ten countries and regions.

Moreover, the Third Month Street Fair is also an occasion for love. In Dali, there is a famous place for people in love to visit, the Butterfly Lake. A romantic story said a young couple, after going through all the hardships, jumped into the lake simply to keep their love alive and transformed into butterflies. In the 1950s, a movie based on the story, *Five Golden Flowers*, was very popular across China. Today, many Chinese still talk about the movie and hum its theme song.

Double Third Singing Carnival

Name: Double Third Singing Carnival for the Zhuang people
Date: the third day of the third lunar month

Liu Sanjie, the "Queen of singers" in Zhuang legends.

Zhuang is China's largest minority group with a population of about 16.2 million according to the fifth national census in 2005. The majority of them live in Guangxi Zhuang Autonomous Region and Yunnan province, and the rest are scattered in Guangdong, Hunan, Guizhou and Sichuan provinces. The Zhuang language used by the Zhuangs is a language branch of the Sino-Tibetan language family. In 1955, China developed and popularized a Zhuang language based on Latin alphabets

Singing Carnival at the Third of the Third Lunar Month is the traditional festival for the Zhuang nationality as the ethnic groups is particularly good at singing. The area where they live is known as the "Seas of Songs" or the "soil floored with piano keys." The Zhuangs, women and men alike, all begin to learn singing at the age of four or five. They sing of love, of play, of work, of sadness, of happiness, of celebration and of mourning. They sing to urge guests to drink at parties and to urge the gods to send rain for the crops. The Zhuangs even challenge each other's wit with antiphonal songs. The best known singers like Liu Sanjie, and Huang Sandi in the Zhuang's history are crowned the "Queen of Singers" and the "King of Singers."

Once in a while, the Zhuang people would gather together to **sing songs at the Singing Carnival**, usually at the third of the third lunar month. Research shows that there are 640 meeting sites for the Zhuangs in Guangxi. The Zhuangs would also meet at Spring Festival, Mid-Autumn or one month after the birth of a child. Even temporary singing meet will be staged when they are on the way to the trading market.

There are songs sung at different occasions. During the "singing meet in the day," young people will gather outdoors in the vast fields singing in a move to seek for the other half. During the "night singing meet," the songs are usually about work, life or history knowledge. The songs sung at different occasions can never be confused, especially at the time of marriage ceremony, worship, and funeral.

At the third of the third lunar month, the Zhuangs from around the area stretching up to hundreds of *li* (two *li* amount to one kilometer) would all dress up to meet to sing. Usually, lads and lasses will stand opposite and lasses will probe lads' character and talent through singing. Men would bring gifts to the women they desire, and women would throw embroidered balls tied with gifts back to the man with who they fall in love.

At some singing meets, people will bring colored eggs. With

Singing folk songs.

an egg in hand, young man will try to touch the egg grabbed in the hand of the woman he has a crush on. The woman, if like the man, will agree for the man to knock on her egg. If not, she would just grab the egg tight, which means: man, no chance for you.

Sometimes, **singing competition** will be held between villages. For instance, Village A will send a silk ball to Village B and challenge it in a folk song competition. According to rules, Village B can only return the ball when it wins the game. If Village B loses in the competition, the embroidered silk ball will just stay. There will competitions in the following years until Village B Wins.

Longduan Street Festival

Name: *Longduan* Street Festival for the Zhuang people
Date: in the third lunar month

*L*ongduan Street is a grand festival popular among the Zhuangs in Guangnan and Funing areas in Yunnan Province. Held in the third lunar month, the fair attracts tens of thousands visitors every year.

The "street" here actually refers to field dam, and the festival

Zhuang opera.

calls on the people to gather in the vast fields. The festival lasts for three to five days, during which young people will seek mates. There are also activities including singing, dancing and trading.

During the festival, the Zhuangs will put on the traditional **Zhuang opera** on a provisional open theater. With the noise of firecracker and the beat of gongs and drums, the opera attract flocks of visitors.

Young people are the most vibrant group during the festival. They come to know each other by dancing and singing together and even vote for "the man of the year" and "the woman of the year" according to their looks and talents.

When a young man has a crush on a woman, he would fire a question by singing, and if the woman likes him too, she would take the question. The **singing conversation** will continue through the whole night until dawn. Men will give jewelry, cosmetics or even money to women they like, and women would give food and shoes made in cloth in return. The festival is a great opportunity for the Zhuangs to express their feelings of love and look for their life partner.

During the festival, the villages are all packed with visitors. Some of them sell daily necessities and agricultural by-products. The trading volume increases every year.

Knife-Pole Festival

Name: Knife-Pole Festival for the Lisu people
Time: the eighth day of the second lunar month

The Lisu, with a population of about 634,900, mainly live in concentrated communities in Nujiang Lisu Autonomous Prefecture in Yunnan Province. There are also small groups scattered in Sichuan Province.

According to historical records, the ancestors of the Lisu once lived along the banks of Jinsha River and Yalong River. Between the 15th and 19th century, they gradually migrated into the drainage areas of the Nu and Lancang rivers. The Lisu has their own language which is a branch of Tibeto-Burman language group.

The Lisu people mainly engage in agriculture. Hunting also plays an important role in their life. The Lisu people are well known for their hospitality and unique etiquette.

The annual Knife-Pole Festival on the eighth of the second lunar month features a physical contest with a history stretching back to hundreds of year. It aims to memorialize a Han hero who was sent by the Ming government and managed to drive away other ethnic groups that intruded into the Lisu area. On the eighth, the hero named Wang Ji was killed by traitors on his way back to Beijing, then capital of the Ming Dynasty.

The Knife-Pole Festival then became the exclusive and traditional festival of the Lisu ethnic group. On that day, people all dressed up and went in flocks to watch various activities including "**Climbing Knife Pole**" and "**Diving into Fire Sea**."

The performers are jumping and dancing over burned coal bare-footed and half-naked, imitating behaviors of animals. They even brush some coals over their body and rub coal balls in hand. The "fire wash" is meant to fend off all the possible disasters and troubles in the new year.

Other performers put on red clothes and red turban. They strided up to a knife ladder which measures 20 meters long and was tied with 36 edged knives. They kneeled down in front of a picture of Wang Ji, drank off a bowl of wine prepared for them and began climbing the knife ladder. The first who reached the top will be hailed with applause and fire cracks. Surprisingly, these men returned to the group safe and round, not with even the slightest scratch.

The exciting and special memorial ceremony

Climbing the Knife Pole.

117

has been officially designated as the traditional festival for the Lisu people.

New Rice Festival

Name: New Rice Festival for the Va people
Date: in the middle of the eighth lunar month

The Va people live mainly in southwestern Yunnan Province with a population around 396,600. The Va people call themselves "*A Va*," which literally means people who live on the mountains. The majority of the Va people are very good at singing and dancing. In some regions, the Va people are followers of Buddhism and Christianity.

The New Rice Festival is the Va people's favorite, and autumn, during which the festival is held, is their busiest season. Every morning, sounds of pounding corns can be heard on the mountains.

For the start of the festival, the Va people pick some corns that has just become ripe and bring them home. The corns are pounded into rice which was cooked and filled into seven bowls, each with a big piece of meat on it. The seven bowls of rice are served up with seven bowls of wine for the God of Heaven, Earth, Mountain, Corn, and their ancestors respectively. Seven incenses are also burned before an old respectable man begins praying. Then the new rice was sent to aged people and kids. The Va people consider the old and the kids as the "cleanest people" in the world. The ritual just symbolizes their worship for god and ancestors, and respect for the old and love for kids.

After the dusk falls, the Vas gathered surrounding a fire and started singing all over the night. If a visitor comes from afar, the host will offer him with his best wine, which was brewed by themselves, and best chicken rice.

The Va people are well known for their hospitality, and the etiquette with wine is most notable.

The host will have a sup first, brush the bamboo cup with his right hand and pass the cup with both his hands to the guest.

Va women are pounding rice.

The guest is supposed to take the wine with his right hand, with his palm upside, and express his gratitude. After having a sup just like the host did, the guest will pass the cup to others as the same way the host did. All people **sup the wine** in turn, using the same cup no matter how many guests are there.

For their rules, guests are not supposed to touch their head or ears in the process. They also should not give gifts and cigarettes to girls who might be family of the host, because the act suggests mate seeking in the Va's world.

On the second day of the festival, young men all go out to maintain the roads on which the new corns will be trucked into the villages. Women are busy cleaning houses. The third day and last day of the festival also features love seeking. After the three-day festival, the Va people formally begin their autumn harvest.

Harvest Ceremony

Name: Harvest Ceremony for the Gaoshan People
Date: the fifth day of the eighth lunar month

The Gaoshan people has a population of 400,000, most of which live in the central mountain areas as well as the Zonggu Plain and Lanyu Island east of Taiwan. There are also some 4,500 Gaoshan people scattered in Fujian, Beijng, Shanghai and Jiangsu. They speak Gaoshan language but write in Chinese since their language has no written forms.

Gaoshan people practice primitive religion, believing in animatism and worshiping heaven, nature and spiritual beings. Some of them are converted to Christianity when it was brought to China. Their traditional festivals are all religious and basically take the form of offering sacrifices. The typical ceremonies include Cultivation Ceremony, Seeding Ceremony, Weeding Ceremony, Harvest Ceremony, Ancestor's Spirit Ceremony, Fishing-and-Hunting Ceremony, etc. Among them, the Harvest Ceremony is celebrated by all Gaoshan people and is the most important one.

119

The annual Harvest Ceremony of the Gaoshan people is equivalent to the Spring Festival of the Han people. It is held in the harvest season, usually in the eighth lunar month. Everyone, old and young, put on their festival best: women wear flowers, brooch, earrings and bracelets; men wear feather hats (or insert two or three bird feathers in hair) and tie bronze bells to their waist belts. Those younger prefer small bells fastened around their ankles. People eat meat, drink wine, sing and dance, totally

*Grand Harvest
Ceremony.*

immersed in the happiness of the festival.

Dancing and singing is a vital criterion for young people to pick up their mates. When a girl falls in for a boy, she would go up to dance with him, and let the expressive steps do the speaking. If a boy is adept at farming, singing and dancing, he would find more than two girls surrounding him. The mass dance, called "**Hand-in-Hand Dance**," features a combination of singing and dancing without instrumental accompaniment.

121

The time-honored and widely popular "Hand-in-Hand Dance" has been entertaining the Gaoshan people for over one thousand years, as a daily recreation or as a special treat on occasions. Led by a talented singer, the participants sing and dance in one or several circles. The lyrics always pay homage to ancestors or legendary heroes. It is spectacular scene when hundreds or even thousands of people are singing aloud and dancing in uniform steps. Some men in excitement would bend down till their feather hats touch the ground before they rise up again. The intoxicated audiences just can't wait to join in them.

Huijia Festival

Name: *Huijia* Festival for the Koreans
Date: varies in different areas

There are an estimated 1.92 million Chaoxian (Korean) people living in China's northeastern provinces of Heilongjiang, Jilin and Liaoning with the rest scattered in the Inner Mongolia Autonomous Region and some cities including Beijing, Shanghai and Hangzhou. Those who live in the Yanbian Korean Automomous Prefecture in Jilin Province speak and write Korean while those who live together with the Han people

Proposing a toast to the aged men.

simply use Chinese.

Basically, the Korean minority celebrate the same festivals as the Han people which including the Spring Festival, the Mid-Autumn Festival, the Pure Brightness Festival, etc. The Korean people also have three famous household festivals, namely, a baby's first birthday, the *Huajia* Festival (celebrating people's 60th birthday) and the *Huihun* Festival (celebrating the sixtieth wedding anniversary).

The Korean people have a long-standing tradition of respect for the aged. In their daily life, young people should never drink or smoke before old people or walk in front of them. If you have the intention of bypassing them, you have to come up with an excuse politely. When old people come head on you, you have to step aside and give way. Young people should also use all the respectful words when talking to old people.

Huijia literally means people aged over 60, and *Huihun* means old couple who have been married for over 60 years.

Of all the ceremonial banquets held by the Koreans, the **Huijia Banquet** stands as the grandest. On this occasion, all relatives and neighbors will be invited for dinner to express the children's heart-felt gratitude for their parents who gave birth to them and reared them.

Talking about *Huajia* Banquet, there is a story.

Once upon a time, an ancient Korean King imposed a law that all old people aged 60 have to be buried alive. A man surnamed Kim, however, managed to hide his aged father to escape death. Years later, some foreign country threatened to invade Korea unless the king can find correct answers to three questions. The king is desperate as he had no idea what are the answers. However, the young man went to the King and told him all the answers that averted the crisis for the country. The king was astonished when the young man told him that the answers were given by his old father who was supposed to be buried alive. Then the king abolished the ruthless law and held a grand *Huajia* Banquet to commemorate wisdom of old people.

On the day of *Huijia* Festival, the Korean villages are immersed in happiness and jollification. Every family is busy making traditional Korean food like "spank cake," cold noodle and dog meat, etc. The person who on that day came to sixty years old will be dressed up, wear a big red flower on his chest and be seated in the middle with others sitting on both sides. His children, grandchildren and relatives would kneel down in front, offering him wine one after another to show their respect and gratitude.

On this particular day, the Koreans will fully engage themselves in dancing, playing swings and wrestling, all as a result effectively play up the joyful atmosphere in the festival.

The date of the festival varies according to different areas. In Heilongjiang Province, it is held on the 20th or 24th of the sixth lunar month, but in Yanbian Korean Autonomous Prefecture, it is held on the 15th of the eighth lunar month.

Filling-up-the-Storehouse Festival

Name: Filling-up-the-Storehouse Festival for the Manchus
Date: the 25th day of the first lunar month

The Manchu, with a population of 10.7 million, are the second largest minority in China. They are mainly distributed in Liaoning Province and scattered in the rest of the country.

The Manchu has its own language and letters, which belong to the Manchu-Tungusic group of the Altaic language family. Manchu letters were created in the 16th century on the base of Mongolian letters.

China's last feudal dynasty, Qing Dynasty, was built in 1644 by the Manchu. As masses of Manchu people came to settled in the Central Plains since the Qing Dynasty, the Manchu became increasingly assimilated by the Han people through frequent exchanges of trade, culture and life styles. The Manchu gradually adopted the Han language.

Most of the Manchus believe in Shamanism, which holds the view that there are many gods commanding the world.

Manchu and Han basically share the same festivals and holidays, such as the Spring Festival, the Lantern Festival, the Mid-Autumn Festival, etc.

"The marriage of the mouse girl," a colored clay sculpture.

On the 25th of the first lunar month, the Manchus celebrate the Fill-up-the-Storehouse Festival. According to the Manchu, at this time of the year, the storehouses went empty. In order to fill up the storehouses, people have to go to the fields and work. On this day, every family is cooking broomcorn which will be put in a bowl and symbolically placed in the storehouse.

Meanwhile, a toy horse made of broomcorn straws is stuck into the broomcorn. The horse, traditional carrier of corns for the Manchu, is meant to pray for a good harvest in the coming years. Some family will instead make two hoes at the occasion. These rituals are still kept in some villages in Northeastern China.

Munao Festival

Name: *Munao* Festival for the Jingpo people (*Munao* Mass Dance)
Date: the 15th day of the first lunar month

The Jingpo people mainly live in Yunnan Province with a population of 132,000. The Jingpo language is a branch of Sino-Tibetan language family based on Latin letters. The ethnic group believes in primitive religion of multiple-gods. The biggest sacrifice ceremony "*Munao* Mass Dance" has turned into an annual festival: *Munao* Festival.

125

"*Munao* Mass Dance" means all people gather dancing. The *Munao* Festival is kicked off on the 15ᵗʰ day of the First lunar month and lasts for four or five days. The festival mainly features singing and dancing, hoping to invite happiness and felicity in the coming years.

"*Munao* Mass Dance" has a long history. Legend has it that the special singing and dancing style of the Jingpo people originated from God of the Sun. It is said that only the children of the Sun can dance in that special manner. Once, the birds of the Earth participated in the Sun's party and learned the dancing of *Munao*. Later, the birds were dancing in the forests and the ancestors of the Jingpo people went to watch and learned the dancing from them. Surprisingly, after the first dancing and singing in that particular manner, the Jingpo people found the productivity of both human and livestock all significantly improved.

All *Munao* Festival activities are conducted around two *Munao* poles erected in the central of a big square or grassland. The poles measures 20 meters high, and two shining huge swords placed between them symbolizes bravery and persistence of the Jingpo people. According to the Jingpos, people standing on either of the two high platforms set up in front of the poles can foresee into the future.

The most wonderful part of the festival is the scene of chaotic dancing, often participated in by thousands of Jingpo people.

The joyful people in their peculiar traditional clothes are cheering as women waving handkerchiefs and men waving swords. The choreographic steps and sequence sometimes dramatize actions of hunting, farming and their daily life. The sound of traditional flutes and gongs is so loud that it can shake the mountains. The excited Jingpo people will keep dancing, even for two days straight.

Munao *Festival.*

Appendix: Chinese Dynasties

Xia Dynasty	2070 BC-1600 BC
Shang Dynasty	1600 BC-1046 BC
Western Zhou Dynasty	1046 BC-771 BC
Spring and Autumn Period	770 BC-476 BC
Warring States Period	475 BC-221 BC
Qin Dynasty	221 BC-206 BC
Western Han Dynasty	206 BC-AD 25
Eastern Han Dynasty	AD 25-AD 220
Three Kingdoms Period	AD 220-AD 280
Western Jin Dynasty	AD 265-AD 317
Eastern Jin Dynasty	AD 317-AD 420
Southern and Northern Dynasties Period	AD 420-AD 589
Sui Dynasty	AD 581-AD 618
Tang Dynasty	AD 618-AD 907
Five Dynasties Period	AD 907-AD 960
Northern Song Dynasty	AD 960-AD 1127
Southern Song Dynasty	AD 1127-AD 1279
Yuan Dynasty	AD 1271-AD 1368
Ming Dynasty	AD 1368-AD 1644
Qing Dynasty	AD 1644-AD 1911
The Republic of China	AD 1912-AD 1949

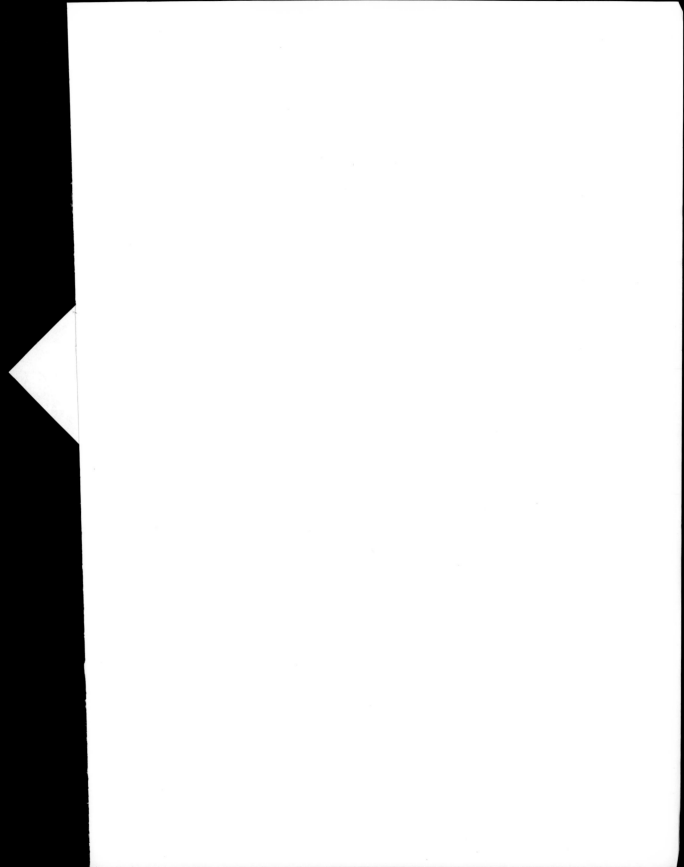

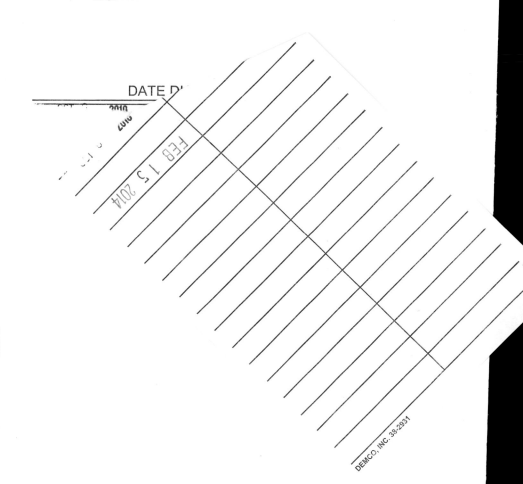

DATE D'

FEB 1 5 2014

DEMCO, INC. 38-2931